Project Explore

Student's Book 2

Sylvia Wheeldon

Paul Shipton

OXFORD
UNIVERSITY PRESS

Based on an original concept
by Tom Hutchinson

Contents

Contents 3

Introduction

A Moving house

YOU FIRST! Imagine your dream house. What rooms has it got? What's in your bedroom? Tell the class.

1 a 🔊 **1.02** ▶ Read and listen. Where do you think Jed is from?

1

Jed	Hi Grandma. We're here in the UK. Finally!
Grandma	How was your flight?
Jed	It was very long. 23 hours.
Grandma	It's a long way, Jed!
Jed	What time is it there?
Grandma	It's nine o'clock in the evening.
Jed	It's ten o'clock in the morning here. Weird!
Grandma	I know!…Are you OK, love?
Jed	No, I'm not OK, Grandma. I don't like moving house. I really don't like leaving my school and my friends. And I hate leaving you!

2

Grandma	I know, love. But you can make new friends.
Jed	I hope so.
Grandma	Have you got a nice bedroom?
Jed	It's big. Look.
Grandma	You've got a great room there. That's a lot of boxes and empty shelves!
Jed	I know! That's another reason why I can't stand moving.
Grandma	What's the house like?
Jed	It's very different. Come on, let's have a tour.
Grandma	Ooh, exciting!

3

Jed	So this is the living room…
Grandma	Nice. It's…
Jed	Oh, we've got a visitor. There's a girl outside the front door!
Grandma	Interesting! How old?
Jed	Not sure. I think she's my age.
Grandma	Even better! Go and see who she is.
Jed	Grandma!
Grandma	Go on! Call me back later.

b Answer the questions.

1 Where is Jed?
2 What time is it there?
3 What's Jed's opinion on moving house?
4 Why does his grandma want Jed to talk to the girl?

2 a Spoken English **What do these expressions mean? How do you say them in your own language?**

 Finally! | Weird! | I hope so. | Ooh, exciting! | Not sure.

b Work with a partner. Practise the dialogues.

3 a Who do you think the girl is?

b 🔊 **1.03** ▶ Listen and check.

4 Over to you! **Work with a partner. Answer the questions.**

1 Why does Lily mention a fairy?

2 What does Jed think about Lily?

3 Who are you close to in your family? Why?

Look! Revision *have got*

Find this example in the story, then find two more examples.

You've got a great room there.

What are the forms of *have got*? When do we use it?

5 Imagine useful or strange things that you have in your bag. Work in groups and add one thing every time.

> In my bag I've got a sandwich, but I haven't got a hairdryer.

> In my bag I've got a sandwich and a hairdryer, but I haven't got a skateboard.

> In my bag I've got a sandwich, a hairdryer and a skateboard, but I haven't got an umbrella...

Grammar *like / don't like / hate + -ing*

6 a **Complete these sentences from the text. Find one more example.**

I ___ house! I really ___ my school and my friends. And I ___ you!

b **Read and complete the rule with verbs from the story.**

☞ We use the *-ing* form after *like, love,* ___ , ___ , *don't mind* and *prefer*.

Vocabulary *plurals*

7 a **Write the plurals. Find examples in the text.**

Singular		Plural
fairy	-y → -ies	fairies
hour	+ -s	____
friend		____
shelf	-f → -ves	____
box	sh / ch / x / s / ss + -es	____

b **Make these nouns plural.**

> cake   dictionary   glass   leaf   visitor   watch

c **Think of another noun for each plural ending.**

Speaking

8 a Get ready to speak **Match the activities to the pictures. Which do you like?**

1 cycling	6 camping
2 running	7 surfing
3 cooking	8 painting
4 taking photographs	9 playing football
5 dancing	10 playing video games

b **Now ask and answer questions with your partner about the activities. Which do you both like doing? Ask why or why not.**

> Do you like cycling?   No, I don't.

> Why not?   I don't like doing exercise!

c **Change partners. Ask and answer questions about your previous partners.**

> Does Anya like running?   No, she doesn't.

> Why not?   It isn't fun.

d **Tell the class one or two interesting facts about your partner or your partner's partner.**

 EXTRA **Complete these sentences with your own examples. Tell a partner.**

I quite like... I love... I really hate...

B Neighbours

YOU FIRST! Which famous person from another country do you like? Why? Where are they from? Tell the class.

1 a 🔊 **1.04** ▶ Read and listen. What more do you find out about Jed?

Lily	Hey Jed. This is Alfie and this is Elsa.
Alfie	Wow! Is that your surfboard?
Jed	Yes, my parents gave it to me for my 14th birthday.
Alfie	Cool. When was your birthday?
Jed	It was on 22nd April.
Lily	Happy birthday – for last month.
Elsa	So you'll be in our year at school?
Jed	I guess so.

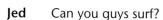

Jed	Can you guys surf?
Alfie	No, we can't. But you obviously can.
Jed	Yes, I can. I love it. I don't know where I can surf in England.
Elsa	Not in Oxford. But you can surf in Cornwall.
Jed	OK! How can I get to Cornwall?
Elsa	You can go by train. It takes about five hours.
Jed	Oh.
Lily	Her memory's great for weird facts...
	Hey, let's show Jed an Oxford kind of water sport.

Jed	What is *that*?
Lily	*That* is punting.
Elsa	You stand at the back of the punt and push it with a pole.
Alfie	It's very relaxing.
Lily	Well, relaxing for *us*. We sit in the boat and you push.
Jed	Oh, very funny...
Elsa	Can you stand on a surfboard?
Jed	Of course I can!
Elsa	Then you can stand on a punt.
Jed	OK. I hope you guys can swim, that's all I can say!

b Are the sentences true (T) or false (F)?

1 Jed is the same age as Lily and her friends.

2 Jed wants to surf in England.

3 He can surf near Oxford.

4 He loves punting.

2 a Spoken English What do these expressions mean? How do you say them in your own language?

 Hey! I guess so. Oh. Oh, very funny. ...that's all I can say!

b Work in a group. Practise the dialogues.

3 a What does Jed think of his new friends? How do you think he's feeling now?

b 🔊 **1.05** ▶ Now listen and check your ideas.

4 Over to you!

1 Do you think Jed is lucky? Why?

2 Do you like making new friends? Do you find it easy or difficult? Why?

Look! Revision *can / can't*

Find this example in the story, then find six more examples.

Can you guys surf?

What are the forms of *can / can't*? When do we use them?

5 Work with a partner. Ask and answer questions about these abilities.

cook a meal   ride a horse   play squash punt   sing   speak French   surf

Can you surf?   Yes, I can. / No, I can't.

Grammar Revise pronouns

6 a Complete the sentences from the text.

Is that ____ surfboard?

Well, relaxing for ____ . ____ sit in the boat and ____ push.

👉 Which is a(n) ...pronoun?

...subject ...object ...possessive

b Complete the chart with pronouns. Use the text and your dictionary to help you.

Pronouns		
Subject	Object	Possessive
I	____	____
you	____	____
____	him	____
she	her	____
it	____	its
we	____	____
____	them	their

Vocabulary Dates and months

January, February, ...

7 a Say the months around the class.

b 🔊 **1.06** Listen and say the correct month.

c Find the birthday in the text. How do we say it?

Look!

We say *the 11th of June*. But we write *11th June*.

d Go round the class asking 'When's your birthday?' Then organize yourselves in a line from January to December.

Listening and Speaking

8 a Look at the table. Fill in what you know already.

b 🔊 **1.07** Listen to Lily and Jed's conversation. Complete the table.

	Lily	Jed
Hometown		
Age		
Birthday		
Brothers / Sisters		
Grandparents		
Favourite hobbies		
Favourite sports		

9 a Get ready to speak Write the questions about Jed, using the correct tenses.

Finding out about someone

1 What / name?

2 Where / from?

3 How / old?

4 When / birthday?

5 ...got / any brothers or sisters?

6 ...got / any grandparents?

7 What / like / doing?

8 What sports / can / do?

b In pairs, ask and answer the questions about Jed.

c Change the questions to ask and answer each other. If you know each other well, invent some new information!

Where are you from?   I'm from Mars...

d Tell the class an interesting fact about your partner.

Tanya's from Italy. She loves speaking English!

 EXTRA Work with a partner. Compare with your partner the birthdays of people in your family. Which birthdays are the closest?

1 Me and my life

1A New friends

YOU FIRST! Who is your oldest friend? What does he or she look like? Tell a partner or the class.

> Hi Grandma! These are my new friends!

Vocabulary Describing people

1 a Who are the people in the photo? Which is the funniest?

> a beard   brown   blue   clever   curly   dark   fair   funny
> freckles   friendly   glasses   kind   long   medium height
> medium length   nice   nice smile   quite tall   quite small   red
> short   shy   sporty   straight   wavy

b In pairs, put the words and phrases in the box in the correct columns. Some can go in more than one column.

hair	eyes	face	body	personality
fair	dark			

c 🔊 **1.08** Listen and repeat. Find as many of the words as you can in the photos.

2 a Complete the beginning of Jed's conversation with Grandma with words from the box.

b 🔊 **1.09** Listen and compare your answers.

Look! Order of adjectives

Describing hair: length, type, colour
She's got long, wavy, dark-brown hair.
Describing eyes: type, colour
He's got big, green eyes.

c Describe the real Alfie and Elsa. Work with a partner and write the descriptions.

d 🔊 **1.10** Listen to the rest of the conversation and compare your ideas.

3 Describe a famous person that your partner should know. Your partner can ask three Yes/No questions to guess who it is.

> She's got long, straight, dark hair and brown eyes. She's medium height with a nice smile. She's funny.

> Is she a pop star?

> No, she isn't.

> **Workbook** page 2, exercises 1–4

Grandma

> Very funny, Jed, but I still don't know who your friends are! Which one is your neighbour, Lily?

> Well, Lily's the girl with the rabbit ears and _glass_. She's actually got _lon_, _glu_, _red_ hair and _brown_ eyes. And she's quite _tall_.

> Oh, OK. And what's she like? She's very _kind_, isn't she?

> Yes, she is. And she's _funny_, too.

Grammar Present simple + adverbs of frequency

4 a 🔊 **1.11** **Read and listen to the dialogue. What does Elsa know about Jed?**

Fred Hey Elsa. Do you know that boy? The tall one with the short, fair hair?

Elsa That's Jed. I don't know him very well. He lives next door to Lily. He's from Australia.

Fred Cool. He looks sporty.

Elsa Oh, he's a surfing champion. In Australia he always surfs every day, in summer and winter. And he often runs with kangaroos, and he sometimes catches crocodiles at weekends. Oh, and he hardly ever sleeps in a bed. He usually stays outside in a tent.

Fred Wow! Does he really do all of that?

Elsa No, of course he doesn't. You believe anything, Fred.

Fred No, I do not!

Elsa He's funny and friendly. Go and talk to him. Or are you shy?

Fred No, I'm not!

b **Find the present simple verbs in the dialogue.**

c **Complete the chart with the correct forms of know.**

➕	I / you / we / they	know	him.
	He / she / it	¹____	
➖	I / you / we / they	don't ²____	him.
	He / she / it	³____ ⁴____	
❓	⁵____ I / you / we / they	⁷____	him?
	⁶____ he / she / it		

d **Choose the correct alternative to complete the rule.**

👉 We use the present simple to talk about:

a things happening now.

b habits and regular activities.

5 a **Complete the chart with adverbs of frequency from the dialogue.**

0%	→		100%
never ____	____	____ ____	always

b **Write the questions in the correct form.**

1 you / play football?

2 your mum or dad / drive / to work?

3 your friends / listen / to music?

4 your teacher / give / you homework?

c **Ask and answer the questions with a partner. Use adverbs of frequency.**

Do you play football?

No, I don't. I never play football!

▶ **Workbook** page 3, exercises 5–7

Writing

6 a Get ready to write **Complete the description with the words in the box.**

concerts eyes good hair medium
music smile usually

One of my best friends   is Ryan. He's ¹___ height with dark, straight ²____ and brown ³____ . He's got freckles and a nice ⁴____ . He's very friendly. He's a ⁵____ student and he ⁶____ works hard at school. He loves ⁷____ and in his free time he plays the drums. He sometimes plays in ⁸____ at school.

▶ **Workbook** page 3, exercises 8–9

b **Write a description of a famous person or classmate. Do not include their name.**

1 What does he / she look like?

2 What is he / she like?

3 What does he / she do?

c **Can your partner guess who it is?**

EXTRA 📋 **Work with a partner.**

Student A Draw a funny face in your notebook. Don't let your partner see it! Describe your drawing.

Student B Draw the face you hear your partner describe.

Look at your pictures. Are they the same? Now swap!

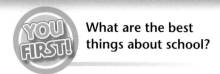

1B New school

YOU FIRST! What are the best things about school?

Vocabulary School and school subjects

1 a Look below. How many things in the picture can you name in one minute?

b Match the words in the box to the picture. Which words are new for you?

> bookshelf   clock   coursebook   dictionary   interactive whiteboard
> notebook   paint   pen   pinboard   projector   ring binder   ruler   tablet
> timetable   waste-paper basket

c 🔊 **1.12** Listen and check. Listen again and repeat.

d Work with a partner. Point to something in the picture or the room. Your partner says the word.

2 🔊 **1.13** Match the school subjects to the definitions. Listen and check.

> Art   Biology   Chemistry   English
> Geography   History   IT   Maths
> PE   Physics

In this subject, you learn about...

1 the language of the UK and USA.
2 how numbers work.
3 countries of the world.
4 important periods in the past.
5 the natural world.
6 sport and health.
7 computers.
8 painting and design.
9 what everything is made of.
10 how things move and make energy.

3 🔊 **1.14** Listen to the conversation. Whose timetable is this? Sarah's or Scott's?

	9.00	10.30	12.00	1.00	2.00
Monday	English	Maths		Biology	Chemistry
Tuesday	History	Geography		Physics	Chemistry
Wednesday	IT	Maths	Lunch	PE	Art
Thursday	English	Geography		Art	Biology
Friday	History	IT		PE	Physics

4 a Draw a timetable like the one above. Put each subject from exercise 2 in twice. Do not show your partner.

b Now ask and answer questions with your partner. If you have the same class at the same time, shout *Snap!*

> What have you got on Monday at nine o'clock?

> I've got Maths at nine o'clock. What about you?

▶ **Workbook** page 4, exercises 1–3

Grammar Present continuous

5 a 🔊 **1.15** Read and listen to the text messages. What are Alfie's problems?

Amy

What are you doing, Amy?

Hey, why are you texting me in lessons?? I'm studying Maths 😮

My pen isn't working. And I'm not feeling well. I'm very hungry 🍎 !!!

I'm trying to write about Shakespeare but I'm BORED!!! 😴 😴 😴

That's because you aren't concentrating. AND you're interrupting me! 😡

Soz 😄 😄

See you at lunch? Are they cooking pizza today?

Yes! I can smell it! 😍 🎉

Great! Oops, my teacher's watching me! 😨

b Find the present continuous forms in the text messages. Complete the sentences with the correct forms.

1 I ____ studying Maths.
2 You ____ interrupting me!
3 My teacher ____ watching me!
4 I ____ feeling well.
5 You ____ concentrating.
6 My pen ____ working.
7 ____ they cooking pizza?
8 What ____ you doing?

c Complete the table with the correct forms.

➕	I	¹____ studying.
	You / We / They	²____ interrupting.
	He / She / It	³____ watching me.
➖	I	'm not feeling well.
	You / We / They	⁴____ concentrating.
	He / She / It	⁵____ working.
❓	Am	I interrupting you?
	⁶____	you / we / they cooking pizza?
	Is	he / she / it working?

d Choose the correct alternative to complete the rule.

👉 We use the present continuous to talk about:
  a activities happening now.
  b habits and regular activities.

6 a Look at the picture of the classroom on page 10 for two minutes. Close your books.

b Work with a partner. Remember what the students are doing. Then look and check.

Two students / Celina and Amy are playing cards.

➤ **Workbook** page 5, exercises 4–5

Listening

7 🔊 **1.16** Listen to four dialogues. What subjects are the students studying? What are they doing? Make notes and compare with a partner.

	subject	doing?
1		
2		
3		
4		

➤ **Workbook** page 5, exercise 6

Speaking

8 a Get ready to speak Work with a partner. What are the differences between these two pictures?

Student A Go to page 86.

Student B Go to page 87.

Look at your picture and make notes about what the people are doing.

b Ask and answer questions to find the differences. These verbs might be useful:

clean   close   organize   pin   put   throw   tidy   write

What are Josh and Sam doing in your picture?

They're writing the date on the whiteboard. Are they doing the same in your picture?

No, they aren't. In my picture, they're...

 EXTRA What are people in your class or in the school doing right now? Write sentences. Compare ideas with a partner.

1C New home

YOU FIRST! Imagine your ideal place to live. What's it like? What are you doing right now in this place? Tell your partner.

Reading and Speaking

1 a Look at the webpage posts. What places do you think you can see in the photos?

b Look at the words in the box below. Can you connect any of the words to the places in the text? Look quickly at the posts to check.

> cold   dangerous   mountains
> old   rainforest   wildlife

2 a Work with a partner.

Student A   Read the text about Chantal.

Student B   Read the text about Dwayne.

b Ask and answer the questions about your partner's text.

1 Where is he / she from? What is it like?

2 Where does he / she live now?

3 What are the differences between the places?

4 In the photo, what activity is he / she doing?

5 How does he / she feel about the move?

6 Can you give one more piece of information from the text?

c Which of the four places do you think is the best and the worst to live in? Why? Discuss with a partner.

> **Workbook** page 6, exercise 1

Kids on the move

> Are you living in a new place? How does it compare to your old home? Share your experiences here!

A

Hello, I'm Chantal and I'm from Falaise in the north of France – most of my family live there. It's small, friendly and very old. But now I'm living in Panama City, South America. It's on the other side of the world! It's a huge, modern city. We're staying here for two years because my parents have good jobs. They work in a big bank in the centre and I go to a French school.

This city has got a forest! Today, we're visiting the Rainforest Discovery Center and at the moment I'm taking photos of all the colourful birds that are flying around in the trees. I often take photos of the amazing wildlife. I miss France, but I like it here – I think it's exciting.

B

I'm Dwayne from Chicago, USA. You can see that Chicago is a huge, busy city and the people are always rushing around. It's very noisy and some parts can be dangerous.

My new home is in Bergen, Norway. My dad has a new job at the university. The winter here is usually very cold and the nights are very long. In this photo, I'm skiing to school! Weird! It's relaxed and quiet here. Most people speak English, but I'm learning Norwegian in my new school because I need to understand it. I have lessons every day. At the moment, I really miss my old home – the way of life is so different here. But it's starting to feel normal. I really want to go to the mountains to learn to snowboard!

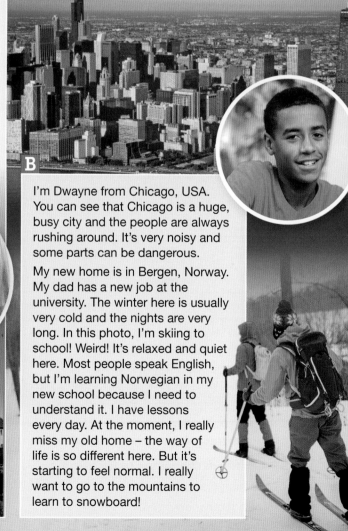

Grammar

Present simple and continuous; stative verbs

3 a Complete the sentences from the web posts. Which is present simple and which is present continuous?

Today we ____ the Rainforest Discovery Center.

They ____ in a big bank in the centre and I ____ a French school.

b Find all the examples of these tenses in the web posts.

c Complete the rules with *now*, *habits*, and *regular*.

☞ We use the present simple to talk about ____ and ____ activities.

We use the present continuous to talk about activities happening ____ and temporary activities.

d Match these expressions to the two tenses. Find some examples in the text.

today   now   usually   every day

present simple   present continuous

always   often   in this photo   at the moment

4 a Find these verbs in the text again. Which tense are they? Which verbs can you *not* find?

☞ Stative verbs:

have got   know   like   love   need

think   want

b Complete the rule with *an activity* and *a state*.

☞ We don't normally use the continuous tense with these verbs because they describe ____ not ____ .

5 Complete the sentences with the same verb in the correct form.

1 a My mum ____ (work) in a bank. She enjoys it.

  b At the moment, he ____ (work) hard for his exams.

2 a Where ____ you ____ (go) now? Can I come?

  b They often ____ (go) by bus to school.

3 a I ____ (take) the dog for a walk now. I'll be back soon.

  b My dad ____ (take) me to drama club every Saturday.

4 a In the summer, I ____ (play) tennis every day.

  b She ____ (play) really well in this match. I think she's going to win!

▶ **Workbook** page 6, exercises 2–4

Mornington

Listening

6 a 🔊 **1.17** Listen. What does Jed usually do in Australia at these times? What is Jed doing now in England? Complete the table.

	Usually in Australia	Now in England
8.15		
12.00		
4.30		
7.00		

b What other information do you remember? Tell the class.

▶ **Workbook** page 7, exercises 5–7

Speaking

7 Get ready to speak Work in a group. Imagine you're doing an activity but do not say what it is. The group asks Yes / No questions to guess the activity. How many questions do you need?

Do you do it often?   Yes, I do.

Do you do it in the morning?   Yes, I do.

Are you having breakfast?   No, I'm not.

Do you do it at home?   No, I don't.

Are you going to school?   Yes, I am!

Role-play. Work with a partner. Pretend you are interviewing Jed for the school magazine. Ask him questions. Take turns.

Do you find it easy or difficult to make new friends?

1 a 🔊 **1.18** ▶ **Read and listen. How do you think Jed feels?**

Lily Hi Jed! How are you getting on?

Jed OK, thanks, Lily. What are you up to?

Lily I'm going to the café.

Jed Can I tag along?

Lily Sure! How was school today?

Jed It was… OK.

Lily Come on. I'll buy you a milkshake.

Jed Thanks, Lily.

Lily Hi, Mr Clarke. This is Jed. From Australia. He's new here.

Mr Clarke Nice to meet you, Jed. How are you getting on?

Jed Erm, good, thanks.

Lily Could I have a strawberry milkshake, please?

Mr Clarke Of course. Same for you, Jed?

Jed Actually, it's a bit cold for milkshakes! May I have a hot chocolate, please?

Mr Clarke No problem.

Alfie Guys! Want to join us?

Lily This is Fred. …Sorry, guys, could I get this?

Jed Go right ahead.

Lily Oops!

Fred Awesome!

Alfie Nice save, Jed!

Fred Hey, Jed, do you play football?

Jed A little bit. I play more rugby. But I love football.

Alfie Can you play tomorrow morning? We need another player.

Jed Sure!

b Are the sentences true (T) or false (F)?

1 Jed asks if he can go with Lily to the café.

2 Mr Clarke is Jed's new school teacher.

3 He orders a strawberry milkshake.

4 He doesn't like football.

2 a Spoken English **What do these expressions mean? How do you say them in your own language?**

Can I tag along?   Want to join us?

A little bit.   Awesome!   What are you up to?

b Work in a group. Practise the dialogues.

▶ **Workbook** page 8, exercise 1

3 a What do you think happens with Jed and the football team? How can it help Jed?

b 🔊 1.19 ▶ Now listen and check your ideas.

4 Over to you! Work with a partner. Answer the questions.

1 How is Jed feeling at the moment?

2 Is it normal to feel like that?

3 Is joining a sports team a good way to make friends? Why? / Why not?

Everyday English

Asking for and giving permission

5 a Look at the information. Which of the examples below can you find in the story?

Asking for permission

Informal	More formal
Can I...?	Could I..., please?
Could I...?	May I..., please ?

Giving permission

Informal	More formal
Sure.	Of course.
Go right ahead.	No problem.

Refusing permission

I'm sorry, no.

I'm sorry, that's not possible.

b 🔊 1.20 Listen and repeat.

▶ **Workbook** page 8, exercises 2–3

Pronunciation The sounds /s/ /z/

6 a 🔊 1.21 Listen and repeat the words. Put them in the correct column.

> amazing   guys   homesick   lives   miss
> of course   outside   plays   please   thanks   us

/s/	/z/
___	please

b 🔊 1.22 Listen again and check your answers.

c Say these words. Is it /s/ or /z/?

> ask   Australia   easy   fantastic
> friends   girls   possible   refuse   sorry

▶ **Workbook** page 9, exercise 4

Listening and Speaking

7 a 🔊 1.23 Listen to three conversations. What are people asking permission for? Do they get it?

	Permission for what?	Yes or no?	Extra information
1			
2			
3			

b 🔊 1.23 Listen again. What extra information can you remember? Check with a partner.

▶ **Workbook** page 9, exercises 5–7

8 a Get ready to speak Ask permission for these things. Decide if you should be formal or informal.

1 go out on a weekday evening with friends

2 use your parent's bike for the day

3 use the teacher's computer

4 miss school for a day

5 play someone's guitar

6 borrow someone's homework

b Role-play with a partner. Try different expressions. Use this chart to help you:

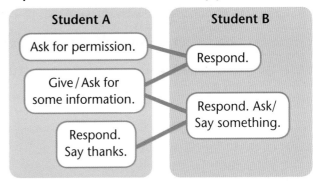

> Can I...?   I'm sorry, no.

c Role-play one of your dialogues for the class.

d Write a new dialogue asking for permission. Use another situation from exercise 8 or use your own ideas. Use one of the Spoken English expressions.

> Could I borrow your computer for my homework, please?   Sure. But what's wrong with your laptop?

 Jed's mum is asking him about school. Work with a partner. Role-play the conversation.

Mum   What's school like, Jed? How are you getting on?

Jed   Fine, Mum. It's...

Vocabulary Describing people

1 Look at the photo and complete the description.

This is my sister.
She's **¹**medium height.
She's got **²**____, straight,
³____ hair and big
⁴____ eyes. She's got
a **⁵**____ smile.
She's kind and friendly.

School subjects

2 Read the definitions and give the school subjects.
1 I'm studying the kings and queens of England.
2 I'm learning how to play basketball.
3 I'm learning about computer programming.
4 I'm learning how to paint a portrait.
5 I'm studying how plants grow.

Classroom objects

3 Complete the dialogues with the words in the box.

> bookshelf   coursebook   dictionary   ruler   whiteboard

1 Can you lend me your ____ , please? I need to draw a straight line.
2 Can I look at your ____ for this lesson? I left mine at home.
3 I need to look up a word. Where's the ____ ?
4 It's on the ____ . I'll get it down for you.
5 Class, look at the ____ and copy the words in your notebooks, please.

Grammar Present simple + adverbs of frequency

4 Rewrite the sentences with the verbs in the correct form and the adverbs in the correct place.
1 I / have / toast / for breakfast   often
2 what / do / you / do / on Saturdays?   usually
3 he / get up / early / at the weekend   never
4 she / play tennis / with me / on Sundays sometimes
5 do / they / go swimming / at the
  leisure centre?   always

Present simple and continuous

5 Complete the sentences with the correct form of the verbs in brackets.
1 It's really hot now so I ____ ice cream. (have)
2 My dad ____ me at drama club every Saturday. (watch)
3 In the summer I ____ to the beach every day. (go)
4 Look! Anna ____ really well at the moment. (play)
5 Paul ____ big green glasses in this photo. He is very funny. (wear)
6 I can't go to the cinema. I ____ my homework now. (do)

Present continuous; stative verbs

6 Complete the dialogue with the verbs in the correct tense.
A What **¹**____ you **²**____ in this shop? (look for)
B I **³**____ to find a pair of shoes. (want)
A Hey, these trainers are nice. **⁴**____ you **⁵**____ them? (like)
B Yes, I **⁶**____ they're nice. (think) But I **⁷**____ boots. (need)

Everyday English

Asking for and giving permission

7 Complete the dialogue with the words in the box.

> ~~can~~   kind   OK   problem   right ahead

A Hi Sam, can I please borrow your tablet for a moment?
B Sure, no ____ . Here you are. What for?
A I need to check the weather. Is that ____ ?
B Go ____ .
A Thanks! You're very ____ .

Learning to learn Using a dictionary 1

8 a A dictionary is in alphabetical order. Put these words in alphabetical order.

> school   personality   friend
> tablet   Geography   curly

b If the first letter is the same, look at the second letter. If they are the same, look at the third letter. Check your answers in a dictionary.

> school   suitcase   study
> standing   Science   straight

▶ **Workbook** pages 10–11, exercises 1–8

My project

What are some important moments in your life so far? Think and make a list.

This is a picture of me. As you can see, I've got curly dark hair, brown eyes and freckles. I'm smiling in this picture. I think I'm friendly, but sometimes I'm a bit shy. I'm not very sporty.

My life in pictures

In this picture, I'm holding my baby brother Emilio. I'm four and he's a day old.

He's very big with a lot of dark hair.

Age 4
my baby brother Emilio's first day!

Age 7
my first bike

In this photo, I'm seven years old. It's my birthday. I'm riding my new bike! It's a present from my grandparents and I love it.

Age 13
third place in school cross country race

AGE

0	1	2	3	4	5	6	7	8	9	10	11	12	13	14

In this photo, I'm 12 years old. I'm with my family and we're on holiday in America. Here we're at a theme park and I'm having a wonderful time!

Age 5
first day at school

Age 9
first day at Girl Guides

Age 11
secondary school

Age 12
holiday in America

In this photo, I'm going to school for the first time. I'm very nervous! I'm holding Mum's arm very tightly. I'm wearing my new school uniform, but I don't like it very much! And I'm carrying my new schoolbag.

1 Find a large piece of paper. Draw a timeline from 0 and mark all the years to now.

2 a Write notes for important times in your life. Try and think of at least six things. Match the notes to the ages on the timeline.

b Read Antonia's timeline. Do you have any of the same things? Are they in the same years?

3 a Look at Antonia's self-portrait. What things does she mention about herself?

b Draw a portrait of yourself and write a description.

4 Look at Antonia's photos. Find three or four photos of you at important times. Then write what you are doing in each of the photos.

5 a Put your project together.

b Present your project to the class. Show your photos and read out the captions. You can use a computer if you prefer. Answer questions from the class.

YOU FIRST! What famous homes do you know? Discuss with a partner.

FAMOUS HOMES

THE WHITE HOUSE IS THE HOME OF THE PRESIDENT OF THE USA AND HIS FAMILY.

The White House is in Washington DC and is more than 200 years old. It is very big with 132 rooms and 35 bathrooms. The president's apartment is on two floors. Presidents live there with their families. The White House is also a place for government work. A lot of the rooms are offices. 6,000 people visit it every day!

The ground floor looks like a shopping centre! It has a flower shop, a dentist's, a cinema, a theatre, a games room and even a bowling lane. Outside, the gardens are beautiful. There are a lot of vegetable gardens and there is a famous rose garden. There is also a tennis court, a swimming pool, and even a running track!

BUCKINGHAM PALACE IS THE LONDON HOME OF THE BRITISH ROYAL FAMILY.

Buckingham Palace is more than 300 years old. It is very big with 775 rooms, including 240 bedrooms and 78 bathrooms. There are also 92 offices. About 450 people work at the palace. There are chefs, electricians, gardeners, drivers, cleaners and two people who look after the 350 clocks! Every year over 50,000 people visit the Queen for dinners and garden parties.

Inside the palace there's a cinema, a swimming pool, a doctor's surgery, a post office and a police station. On the walls, there is an amazing collection of art. Underneath the palace, there are a lot of secret tunnels! Outside, the gardens are huge and beautiful. There are tennis courts, a boating lake, and also a helicopter pad.

1 **a** Work with a partner.

Student A Read about the White House.

Student B Read about Buckingham Palace.

b Ask and answer the questions about your famous home.

Where is it?	What happens there?
How old is it?	What is there inside?
Who lives there?	What are the gardens like?
How big is it?	

c What was the most interesting fact in each text?

d Which one would you like to live in? Why?

2 **Over to you!** Which famous homes or buildings are there in your country? Do people still live or work there?

 An unusual home

Is there any style of art or painting that you like? Which famous artists do you know of?

Artists' self-portraits

A The artist is 33 years old in this self-portrait, but he / she doesn't look very well. He / She's wearing ¹____ pyjamas and sitting in front of a red curtain. He / She has got dark ²____ and a moustache and he / she's looking to the right. The artist has also got a black patch over his / her left ³____ . It's a strange picture.

B This artist is 41 years old in this self-portrait. He / She is sitting in his / her room next to a ⁴____ picture. He / She has got very green eyes and is wearing ⁵____ clothes. He / She has got a bandage on his / her right ⁶____ and looks ill. Behind on the right is a ⁷____ and on the left is an empty painting. It's a sad picture.

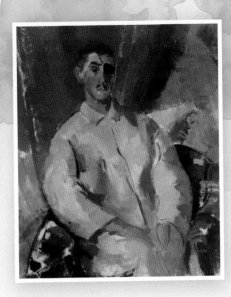

1 a Look at these three famous artists and their self-portraits. Can you match the artists to their paintings and the titles and their styles?

1 Vincent van Gogh 1853–1890 (Dutch)
2 Marie Spartali Stillman 1844–1927 (British)
3 Rik Wouters 1882–1916 (Belgian)

a Self-portrait on a balcony 1874 (Pre-Raphaelite)
b Self-portrait with bandaged ear 1889 (Post-Impressionist)
c Self-portrait with a black eye patch 1915 (Fauve)

b Do you know anything about any of these artists? Can you find out anything about them?

2 a Complete the descriptions with the words in the box.

> ear   eye   hair   light blue
> Japanese   window   winter

b 🔊 1.24 Listen and check.

3 a Look at the third painting. Try and describe it. Use these words.

> balcony   dress   fan   red   smiling

b 🔊 1.25 Listen and compare your ideas.

4 Write a short description of the painting below (or choose a picture that you like). Answer the questions.

Who is in the picture?

How old is the artist in this picture?

Where are they?

What are they wearing?

What is the artist doing?

What's the feeling in this picture?

Elisabeth Le Brun 1755–1842 (French)

Self-portrait with daughter Julie (age 6) 1786 (Neoclassical)

5 Over to you! What do you think? Discuss with your class.

1 Which painting do you find the most interesting? Why?
2 Which style of painting do you prefer?
3 Which painting do you like best and least? Why?

🔊 1.26 ▶ Song *Ugly*

YOU FIRST! What do you like doing when it's sunny and when it's snowing? Make a list and compare with your partner.

Vocabulary Weather

1 a Look at the picture. How many types of weather can you find and name?

b Match the words to the correct weather. How many did you know?

> It's cloudy.   It's cold.   It's foggy.   It's freezing.
> It's hailing.   It's hot.   It's raining.   It's snowing.
> It's stormy.   It's sunny.   It's warm.   It's wet.
> It's windy.   There's a rainbow.

c 🔊 **1.27** Listen and check, then repeat.

d Work with a partner. Cover the words. Point to a number. Ask and answer the questions.

> What's the weather like?   It's hot.

2 🔊 **1.28** Listen to the conversations and write the correct weather.

3 a Make weather flashcards. Draw the 14 different types of weather on pieces of paper. Place the flashcards face down.

b Work with a partner. Take turns to turn over a flashcard and start a conversation.

> It's snowing…
>
> Let's go swimming!   Let's make a snowman!
>
> No way! My turn!   Great idea! Your turn again!

▶ **Workbook** page 12, exercises 1–2

Reading and Grammar

Past simple regular

4 ◀)) **1.29** Read and listen. How did the family survive?

MISSING FAMILY FOUND ALIVE IN THE SNOW

In 2013 in Nevada, USA, two adults and four children survived for two nights in the freezing mountains.

In December 2013, the weather in Nevada was cold but sunny. So, on Sunday 6th, James and Christina Glanton wanted to take their two children and cousins to play in the snow. Early in the morning, they travelled by jeep into the mountains.

But in the afternoon the weather changed. There was a huge snowstorm and the road was dangerous. The Glanton's jeep suddenly stopped in the snow and then it turned over! The family couldn't move, there wasn't a phone signal, and it was freezing. The temperature was –16 degrees! But James had an idea. He used a tyre from the jeep to make a fire. Then they warmed rocks in the fire. At night they all stayed with the warm rocks in the turned-over jeep.

On Monday morning at 8 o'clock, 200 people started to look for the missing family. There were a lot of jeeps and two helicopters. The rescuers were very worried. People usually can't survive one night in the mountains in winter. The rescuers listened for tiny mobile phone signals. Then they tried to follow the signals.

On Tuesday at 4 o'clock in the afternoon, the rescuers finally arrived. They were very happy to find the family alive and well!

5 a Look at the highlighted verbs. Complete the rule with *past* or *present*.

☞ We use the ___ simple to talk about events which happened at a time before now.

b Look at the highlighted verbs again. What are the spelling rules?

Base verb	Past simple regular	Spelling rule
survive	survived	+ -d

c Find more examples of past simple regular verbs in the text.

There was / were

6 a Complete the sentences from the text. Find a negative form.

☞ ___ ___ a huge snowstorm and the road was dangerous.
___ ___ a lot of jeeps and two helicopters.

b Write the questions. Then answer them.
1 How many people ___ in the jeep?
2 How many people ___ in the rescue team?

Prepositions of time

7 a Complete these sentences from the text. Find more examples. What are the rules?

☞ ___ Tuesday ___ 4 p.m. ___ the afternoon, the rescuers finally arrived.

b Do these dates and times take *at, in* or *on*?

> autumn   February   16th February   July   12th July
> lunchtime   midday   20th   Wednesday   2017

▶ **Workbook** pages 12–13, exercises 3–7

Speaking and Listening

8 a **Get ready to speak** Work with a partner.
Student A Go to page 86.
Student B Go to page 87.
Look at the pictures for one minute. Then, close your books and describe the pictures to your partner.

> There was a...and there were two...

b 📝 Work together to put the six pictures in order. Write sentences for each picture. Use the words and the correct form of the past simple. Add details if you can.

c ◀)) **1.30** Listen to the story and check your ideas.

 EXTRA Make a sentence about last weekend. Your partner decides if it is true (T) or false (F).

> arrived   liked   listened   played   stopped
> travelled   tried   waited   wanted   watched

YOU FIRST! What do you think daily life is like in the jungle? Who lives there?

Reading

1 Describe what you can see in the photos. What do you think the text is about?

2 a Read the text. Complete the gaps (1–5) with the correct sentences (A–E).

b 🔊 **1.31** Listen and check the order. What do you think of the story?

A In Brazil in 2014, two men came out of the Amazon jungle.

B But life wasn't exactly the same.

C Did life improve for the tribe outside the jungle?

D But why did they leave the jungle?

E After that, 23 more adults and 12 children left the jungle.

The lost tribe

1 _____ Who were they? They didn't have clothes and they didn't speak Portuguese. This was their first visit to our modern world. The photographs of them went viral on the internet.

2 _____ They were all from the Sapanahua tribe. A translator spoke to them, and a Brazilian doctor took care of them. They needed medicine because our illnesses are dangerous to them.

3 _____ Well, they were scared of wild animals and thunderstorms. But they were most scared of other people, because there were a lot of dangerous criminals in the Amazon jungle. So, the Brazilian government gave the tribe new homes beside the river. There they could live in the same way.

4 _____ For the first time, the tribe had clothes, shoes, and other modern things – and they loved them! At first, they didn't understand a camera. Then, minutes later, a ten-year-old boy learned to take photos.

5 _____ Yes and no. They weren't hungry or frightened any more. But they missed the freedom of life in the jungle.

And there are more of these tribes in the Amazon. Are they in danger, too?

Grammar Past simple *be*

4 a Complete the sentence from the text. Then find all the *was / were* examples in the story.

They ___ all from the Sapanahua tribe.

b How do we form negatives and questions? Complete the rules.

☞ To make the past form of *be*, we use ___
or ___ .
For negatives, we use *wasn't* or ___ .
To make questions, we use ___ or *Were…?*

Past simple irregular

c Find the past simple irregular forms of these verbs in the story.

> can   come   give   go   have
> leave   speak   take

Past simple questions and negatives: regular and irregular verbs

5 a Find three negative forms in the past simple. Complete the rule.

☞ To make negatives, we use ___ + base verb.

b Complete the questions from the story.

But why ___ they ___ the jungle?
___ life ___ for the tribe outside the jungle?

c Complete the rules.

☞ To make past simple questions, we use ___ + base verb.

> **Workbook** page 14, exercises 1–3

6 Give the irregular past simple form of these verbs.

> buy   eat   find   hear   run   say   see   think

7 Write the questions about the story. Work with a partner. Ask and answer the questions.

1 …37 people / come / out of the jungle?
2 …they / have / clothes?
3 …they / speak / Portuguese?
4 Why / a doctor / see them?
5 …they / frightened in the jungle?
6 …life / the same outside the jungle?
7 What / the government / give them?
8 …they / like / clothes and cooking things?

> **Workbook** pages 14–15, exercises 4–5

Listening and Speaking

8 a 🔊 **1.32** Listen to people talking about their amazing holidays. Match the names with the places (1–4) and activities (a–d).

Bob

Cleo

Anton

Maria

b Work with a partner. Discuss which trip you think is interesting.

> **Workbook** page 15, exercises 6–7

9 a Get ready to speak Choose one of these places and activities. Imagine you went there. You are now back from your trip. What was it like? Make notes.

> **I went…**
>
> windsurfing at the beach.   horse riding in the country.
> swimming in the lake.   shopping in the city.
> climbing in the mountains.   trekking in the jungle.

b Write the questions. Write two more questions.

1 were   Where   on holiday   you   ?
2 weather   the   like   was   What   ?
3 you   What   do   did   ?
4 did   with   you   do   Who   it   ?
5 Did   interesting   anything   you   see   ?

c Invent more details about your trip in 9a. Work with a partner. Ask and answer the questions above.

d Tell the class an interesting thing that your partner did.

> Jonah saw a tiger in the jungle!

EXTRA Write questions to ask your partner about their best holiday. Ask and answer.

Where did you go on your best holiday?

I went to…

Do you like storms? Are they exciting? Why?/Why not?

Vocabulary

Extreme weather and natural disasters

1 **a** Look at the words. Which do you know? Match them to the definitions.

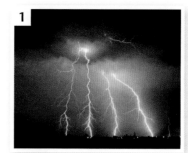

an avalanche   an earthquake
a flood   a hurricane   lightning
a snowstorm   a tornado
a tsunami   a volcanic eruption

a a huge wave of water

b a volcano exploding

c wind that travels in a circle

d electricity in the sky

e too much water

f a lot of snow and wind

g rocks or snow falling down a mountain

h very strong winds

i the earth moving and breaking

b Look at the photos. Match the words to the photos.

c 🔊 **1.33** Listen, check and repeat.

d Work with a partner. Take turns pointing to a photo or saying a definition. Your partner says the word.

2 **a** 🔊 **1.34** Listen to three conversations. Complete the first column of the chart.

b 🔊 **1.34** Listen again. Write the information for the second and third column.

	Disaster	Where	When
Conversation 1			
Conversation 2			
Conversation 3			

3 Look at the map. Where in the world do these natural disasters happen? Can you remember any news stories about extreme weather or natural disasters? Discuss with the class.

➤ **Workbook** page 16, exercise 1

Grammar

4 🔊 **1.35** Look at the photo. What do you think the article is about? Read and listen to the interview and check your ideas.

TEEN SURVIVES
DISASTER

Interview with Scott Gilbert

Interviewer: When and where did the disaster happen?

Scott: It happened two years ago in Oklahoma, USA.

I: Who were you with?

S: I was at home…alone.

I: What happened?

S: It was extremely windy, and then a huge tornado came.

I: How often do you have tornados in Oklahoma?

S: We have them a lot.

I: What did you do?

S: Well, I ran to the bathroom.

I: Why did you do that?

S: So I could hold on to the toilet!

I: And how did you survive the tornado?

S: Well, the toilet is connected underground, so it didn't move.

I: How long were you in the bathroom?

S: I was there for half an hour, I think.

I: Oh no! Were you hurt?

S: No, I was very lucky!

Question words

5 a Complete the question and answer from the interview. What are the question words?

👉 I: ___ and ___ did the disaster happen?

S: It ___ two years ago in Oklahoma, USA.

b Find all of the question words in the interview. Take turns practising the interview with a partner.

👉 When   Where   ___ ___ ___ ___ ___ ___

Adverbs of time

6 Complete the rules with adverbs from the interview.

👉 Adverbs of time tell you when, how long, or how often actions happen.

When?   Today, yesterday, later, last year, a long time ago, ___

How often? Every day, once or twice, sometimes, never, ___

How long? Not long, all day, for a while, for a week, ___

▶ **Workbook** pages 16–17, exercises 2–4

7 a Write questions about last week. Add two more.

1 How often / you / speak English in class / last week?

2 When / you / do / homework / last week?

3 How long / you / study / in the evening / last week?

b Ask and answer the questions with a partner.

▶ **Workbook** page 17, exercise 5

Listening and Writing

8 a Write more questions for Scott.

1 What / you / do / after the tornado stopped ?

2 Why / you / do that ?

3 When / your family / come / back ?

4 How / they / feel ?

5 Where / you all / live / after that ?

6 How long / you / stay there ?

b 🔊 **1.36** Listen to the interview and check your questions. Make notes on the answers.

c Role-play the dialogue with a partner.

▶ **Workbook** page 17, exercises 6–7

9 a *Get ready to write* Complete the first paragraph of the newspaper report with information from Scott's interview in exercise 4.

Two ¹___ ago, in ²___ , USA, teenager Scott Gilbert was ³___ . It was ⁴___ and then ⁵___ . He ran ⁶___ , so he ⁷___ . He ⁸___ because the toilet ⁹___ , so it ¹⁰___ ! He was there ¹¹___ , but he wasn't ¹²___ . He was very ¹³___ !

b Now write a second paragraph about what happened after that. Use information from exercise 8.

EXTRA Choose an extreme weather event or natural disaster. Work with a partner. Discuss how to survive in that situation.

 YOU FIRST! Do you go camping? Do you enjoy it? Why?/Why not?

1 a 🔊 **1.37** ▶ **Look at the photos. What do you think happened? Read and listen.**

1

Elsa   Why did you decide to camp out in that weather?

Lily   Yes, I didn't sleep with the wind and the rain, and I was *inside*.

Jed   Well, we're tough.

Alfie   And very brave.

Elsa   Sure you are… Tell us the story.

Jed   Well, Grandma sent me a tent. She said it was for *all* weather.

Alfie   And we wanted to try it.

Jed   So we put it up… but *someone* didn't hold it down!

Alfie   Well, sorry about that, but *you* didn't ask me to!

Lily   Guys, guys, it doesn't really matter! The story!

2

Jed   Yes, well, the wind blew the tent over the wall…

Lily   Oh no! Into our garden?

Elsa   Oh no! Into Mr Grant's garden?

Lily   Oh, bad luck!

Jed   Exactly, Mr Grant's dog, Albert, was out too.

Lily   Oh, that's a shame. Albert isn't very friendly.

Alfie   No, he isn't. He bit it…

Jed   …and he didn't let go. We pulled and pulled…

Alfie   …in the mud and rain for ages… Hey, it's not funny!

Lily   No, of course it isn't… poor you!

Elsa   Never mind!

Elsa   So, what did you do after that?

Jed   We put the tent back up, got the sleeping bags and went to sleep.

Lily   In the tent? In that weather?

Elsa   All night? Really?

Jed   Oh, yes. We're very brave, Elsa.

Elsa   Hmm…

Lily   That *is* brave.

Alfie   Thank you, Lily.

3

b Are the sentences true (T) or false (F)?

1 The boys decided to try Jed's tent.

2 The weather wasn't very good for camping.

3 The neighbour's dog is called Grant.

4 The camping was successful in the end.

2 a Spoken English **What do these expressions mean? How do you say them in your own language?**

Sure you are…   Guys, guys!   Exactly!   It's not funny!

b Work in a group. Practise the dialogues.

▶ **Workbook** page 18, exercise 1

3 a What do you think of the boys' story? What do the girls think of it? How do you think the story ends?

b 🔊 1.38 ▶ Now listen and check your ideas.

4 Over to you! Work with a partner. Answer the questions.

1 What happened to the tent in the end?
2 How did the boys behave? Were they brave?
3 What was the girls' opinion of the boys in the end?

Everyday English

Expressing sympathy and regret

5 a Look at the useful phrases. Find examples in the story.

1 Bad luck!
2 Oh no!
3 That's a real shame!
4 Never mind.
5 Sorry about that.
6 Poor you.
7 It really doesn't matter.
8 Sorry to hear that.

b 🔊 1.39 Listen and repeat.

▶ **Workbook** page 18, exercises 2–3

Pronunciation The sounds /e/ /iː/

6 a 🔊 1.40 Listen and repeat the words. Put them in the correct columns.

friendly me never real
see teeth tell tent weather
week we'll well

/e/	/iː/
tent	___

b 🔊 1.41 Listen and check your answers.

c Say these words. Is it /e/ or /iː/?

beak bookshelf cheap
desk niece pen please present
police secret sweets

▶ **Workbook** page 19, exercise 4

Listening and Speaking

7 a 🔊 1.42 Listen. Which pieces of bad news do you hear?

a I dropped my phone this morning!
b It rained all the time on holiday.
c I didn't pass my last exam!
d I broke my arm playing tennis on Wednesday.
e We lost the match this afternoon.
f I left my homework on the bus yesterday.

b 🔊 1.42 Listen again. What extra information can you remember? Check with a partner.

▶ **Workbook** page 19, exercises 5–6

8 a Get ready to speak Choose another piece of bad news in exercise 7 or use your own ideas.

b Role-play. Work with a partner. Try different expressions. Use this chart to help you:

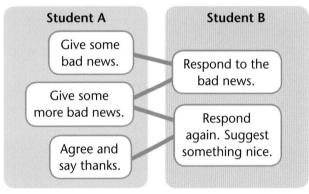

Student A	Student B
Give some bad news.	Respond to the bad news.
Give some more bad news.	Respond again. Suggest something nice.
Agree and say thanks.	

What's wrong?

I dropped my phone this morning!

c Role-play one of your dialogues for the class.

EXTRA What does Jed say to his grandma on the phone about the tent? Finish the conversation.

Jed — Grandma, thank you very much for the tent. But I'm sorry. Something terrible happened to it yesterday...

Grandma — Oh no. What happened?

Jed — Well, ...

Vocabulary Weather

1 Look at the pictures and write the weather.

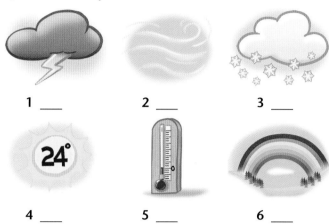

1 ___   2 ___   3 ___

4 ___   5 ___   6 ___

Extreme weather and natural disasters

2 Complete the sentences with the words in the box.

> avalanche   flood   hurricane
> lightning   volcanic eruption

1 The ___ blew the tree down because the wind was so strong.

2 The storm was amazing – the ___ lit up the sky.

3 Mount Etna had another small ___ – there was noise and smoke, but no damage.

4 It rained so much that there was a ___ in the town.

5 There was an ___ in the mountains next to the ski resort and no one could ski.

Grammar Past simple

3 Complete the dialogue with the past simple form of the verbs in brackets.

A Hi Josh! ¹___ you ²___ your holiday? (enjoy)

B Yes, thanks, I ³___ . It was great. (do)

A ⁴___ you ⁵___ good weather? (have)

B Yes, but one day we ⁶___ a storm. (have)

A ⁷___ you ⁸___ any photos? (take)

B Lots. I ⁹___ you some while I was away. (send)

A Oh no! I ¹⁰___ them. I ¹¹___ my phone last week! (not see, lose)

Prepositions of time

4 Choose the correct prepositions to complete the sentences.

1 His birthday was last week _on_ the 22nd.

2 I told you to be here _at_ seven o'clock!

3 Did we go on holiday _in_ June or July?

4 The garden looks best _in_ spring.

5 I sent the email _on_ Tuesday, 11th February.

6 He's always busy ___ weekends.
   _at/on_

Question words

5 Complete the questions, then choose a suitable adverb / adjective to answer them.

> how   long   often   when   where

1 A How ___ did you play football last week?

   B I played *every day / many years ago*.

2 A ___ did you finish your homework?

   B I finished it *later / last night*.

3 A ___ were you yesterday? I didn't see you at school.

   B I was *at home / last year*.

4 A How ___ was the film?

   B It was so long! It was *every day / three hours long*.

5 A ___ was your holiday?

   B It was *brilliant / two weeks long*.

Everyday English

Expressing sympathy and regret

6 Complete the dialogue with the words in the box.

> finish   for you   have to
> never mind   to hear that   wrong

A What's ¹___ ?

B I didn't ²___ my homework and I have to stay in school this afternoon!

A Oh, no. Very sorry ³___ .

B I ⁴___ do it all again.

A ⁵___ . I can wait ⁶___ .

B Thanks!

Learning to learn
Using a dictionary 2

It's a good idea to use a dictionary to help you with new words.

Look at this dictionary extract. Find these things:

> the word   the meaning
> another meaning
> the type of word that it is   an example
> the spellings in different forms

crawl ¹ ³ ⁴
verb (crawls, crawling, crawled)

² 1 to move along on your hands and knees
   2 to move slowly   5   6
   a slug was crawling across the path

▶ **Workbook** pages 20–21, exercises 1–7

My project

YOU FIRST! Which country would you really like to visit? Why?

A country fact file

Brazil

Flag:
Capital: Brasilia
Population: 207.8 million
Currency: Brazilian real
Language: Portuguese
Weather: warm and dry or warm and rainy

BRAZIL is a very large country in South America. It is famous for its huge Amazon rainforest and long Amazon River. It also has a lot of beautiful beaches.

Winter in Brazil lasts for three months from June to August, but it is rarely cold at any time of year. That's why it is such a popular place for holidays. Rio de Janeiro is Brazil's most famous city, and everyone recognizes Sugarloaf Mountain.

For a long time there were only native tribes in Brazil. Then Europeans from Portugal and Spain arrived in Brazil during the 15th century. Eventually, in 1822, it became an independent country.

The Amazon rainforest is disappearing because people are building farms and making fields. More than 20% of the rainforest is now gone. Now people are trying to save the rainforest.

1 a Get ready to write **Choose an interesting country. What interests you about it?**

b Find facts and photos of your chosen country – from home, on the internet, or from books and magazines.

c Find out these facts:

Flag: ____	Currency: ____
Capital: ____	Language: ____
Population: ____	Weather: ____

2 a Plan three short paragraphs. Choose some of the information below to include.

Size
Which continent
What it's famous for
Famous natural features
Famous places
Weather and seasons
Some important dates in its history

b Read the text from Anton's project. Which information has he chosen to include? In which order?

3 Read the Look! box. Find examples in the text.

Look! Time expressions

There are many different expressions to tell us when things happen. Look at the examples. Find them in the text.

Between two points in time, e.g. *from July to September*

Duration, e.g. *for a long time, during, lasts*

Relationship in time, e.g. *then, eventually*

Linkers, e.g. *and, because, also, that's why*

4 a Start writing **Decide how you are going to organize your information and how you are going to lay out your text and pictures.**

b Put your information into sentences and paragraphs.

c Try to use one or two time expressions.

5 a Complete your project **Arrange your information as a large poster with pictures, or make a PowerPoint presentation. Make sure your information is bright and colourful.**

b Put your project on the class wall or show your presentation in class. Read them and discuss. Which country did you learn something new about?

What famous explorers do you know? Tell the class.

Two British
EXPL RERS

DAVID
LIVINGSTONE

was the first European to explore all of Africa.

GERTRUDE BELL

was the first European to explore all of the Arabian desert.

David Livingstone was a missionary and explorer, born in Scotland in 1813. His family was very poor, and from the age of ten he worked from 8 until 6 in a factory. But he studied hard at night and became a doctor. However, he was fascinated by other countries. So, when he was 27, he went to Africa, because no one knew much about it. For 15 years, he travelled on foot all over the country, usually with some servants. He found waterfalls and jungles and made the first maps of the African continent. The expeditions were extremely hard and sometimes he only ate insects. Livingstone was very interested in native tribes. When he returned to Britain, he spoke against slavery. He went back to Africa and died there from malaria when he was 60 years old.

Gertrude Bell was an English adventurer, historian and spy. She was born in 1868 into a rich family and was the first woman to get a first-class degree in history from Oxford University. When she was 24, she made her first trip to the Middle East, and was fascinated by its history and people. For 15 years until 1914, she made trips through the deserts of Arabia with a servant and a tent. She travelled by camel or horse and made the first maps of the region. During WWI she was the first female spy for British Intelligence. After the war she worked for the British government and supported the new nation of Iraq. She always spoke for Arab independence and against British colonialism. She died in Baghdad when she was 57 years old.

1 a Work with a partner.

Student A Read about David Livingstone.

Student B Read about Gertrude Bell.

b Ask and answer the questions about your explorer.

1 When and where was (s)he born?

2 What was his / her childhood like?

3 What was (s)he really interested in?

4 How old was (s)he when (s)he left Britain to explore?

5 How did (s)he usually travel when (s)he was there?

6 How many years (s)he travel for?

7 What did (s)he speak against back in Britain?

8 Where and when did (s)he die?

c What was the most interesting fact in each text?

d Would you like to be an explorer? Why? / Why not?

2 Over to you! Who are the famous historical figures in your country? What are they famous for?

 Robert Falcon Scott

Antarctica

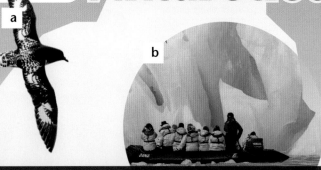

 YOU FIRST! What do you know about Antarctica? Look at the headings in exercise 1 and write your ideas for each one.

1 a Read and check your ideas. Match the photos and headings to the correct paragraphs.

> animals and birds   history of exploration
> population   sea life   tourism   weather

b What new information did you learn? Which two pieces of information do you think are the most interesting?

1 _____

Antarctica is the **COLDEST** continent on Earth. There isn't much rain, but there is a lot of snow and wind. The lowest temperature was on 21 July in 1983 at **−89.2°C!**

2 _____

Nobody lives in Antarctica all the time! The first people to stay there for a while were fishermen in 1786. Now there are about **5,000 SCIENTISTS** and researchers there in the summer.

3 _____

Blue whales, humpback whales, killer whales, penguins and seals live in the sea around Antarctica. **18 TYPES OF PENGUIN** live there. Penguins only live at the South Pole, not the North Pole.

4 _____

There aren't any large animals in Antarctica. Polar bears live at the North Pole. But there are some big snails and a lot of insects. Every spring there are over **100 MILLION SEABIRDS** in Antarctica.

5 _____

During 1907–9, British explorer Ernest Shackleton explored the continent on foot. In 1911, two explorers – a British man named Scott and a Norwegian named Amundsen – raced 1,400 kilometres to the South Pole. Amundsen arrived first. Scott and his team died on the way back.

6 _____

People started to visit Antarctica in 1950. Then the first tourist ships sailed from Argentina in 1969. Now, over **34,000 VISITORS** arrive there every summer.

2 a 🔊 **1.43** Listen to Allie talking about her holiday to Antarctica. Which of the topics from the infographic does she talk about? Number the headings from exercise 1 in the order you hear them.

b Imagine you lived in Antarctica for a week to study wildlife. What did you take with you? What did you see and do? Write a journal entry.

1 🔊 1.44 ▶ Read and listen to the story.

Food and health

3A Food and drink

YOU FIRST! What are your favourite foods? What's your favourite drink? Tell a partner. Do you like the same things?

Vocabulary Food and drink nouns

1 a Cover the words in the box. In pairs, how many items of food and drink can you name?

b Match the words and the pictures. Compare answers with the class. Which five foods are not in the pictures?

bananas carrots cheese chicken chocolate
coffee cola crisps eggs fish fruit juice
grapes ham lamb lemonade milk pasta
potatoes rice sandwiches sausages strawberries
tea tomatoes wholegrain bread yoghurt

2 a Put the words above under the correct headings.

drink	fruit / vegetables	snacks	meat / fish	other
lemonade	grapes	yoghurt	ham	pasta

b 🔊 **2.02** Listen, check and repeat.

3 a 🔊 **2.03** Listen to three conversations. Which food or drink do these people really like? Which do they really dislike?

	Likes	Dislikes	Extra info
Joe			
Ava			
Simon			

b Can you remember one piece of extra information about the food they like?

4 Look at the food and drink in exercise 1. Ask and answer questions with your partner.

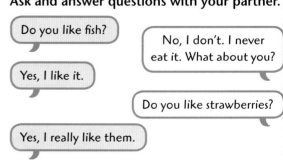

Do you like fish?

No, I don't. I never eat it. What about you?

Yes, I like it.

Do you like strawberries?

Yes, I really like them.

▶ **Workbook** page 24, exercises 1–2

Grammar Countables/uncountables

5 a Read the list. What is it for?

1	crisps	7	tomatoes
2	chocolate	8	sandwiches
3	fruit juice	9	fruit
4	bread	10	bananas
5	ham	11	apples
6	cheese	12	a cake

b 🔊 **2.04** Listen to Lily and Alfie to check your ideas. Which items have they got already? Which items do they need to get?

c Read the rules. Look at the list. Match each word to a rule.

👉 A countable noun has a singular and a plural form:

an egg → two eggs

You can count it with numbers.

An uncountable noun usually hasn't got a plural form, because you can't count it with numbers:

milk → milk

d Look at the food lists. Write *countable* and *uncountable* at the top of the correct list.

____
cheese   chocolate   ham   lemonade   milk

____
banana   egg   sandwich   strawberry

6 📝 Add these items to the correct food lists in exercise 5d.

carrot   coffee   grape
potato   rice   tea

7 Work with a partner. Imagine you are going shopping. Take it in turns to add items to your shopping bag. Remember everything in order!

In my shopping bag there's fruit juice and there are strawberries.

In my shopping bag there's fruit juice, strawberries, and there is cheese.

▶ **Workbook** pages 24–25, exercises 3–5

Listening and Speaking

8 a 🔊 **2.05** Read the menu. Listen. What does Jed order? Why is Lily surprised?

Parkside CAFE

Hot food
Fish and chips	£6.50
Chicken and chips	£5.20
Ham and eggs	£4.99
Pizza	£6.99

Sandwiches
Ham	£3.50
Egg	£2.99
Cheese	£2.99

Desserts
Chocolate cake	£2.25
Strawberry yoghurt	£0.75
Ice cream	£1.75

Drinks
Fruit juice	£1.50
Lemonade	£1.25
Cola	£1.25
Cup of tea	£1.50
Cup of coffee	£2.00
Strawberry/chocolate milkshake	£2.50

b 🔊 **2.05** **Get ready to speak** Complete the dialogue. Listen again and check.

Waitress Can I ¹____ you?

Jed Yes please. Can I have ²____ , please?

Waitress Anything for ³____ ?

Jed Yes, ⁴____ , please.

Waitress OK. And do you want anything to drink?

Jed Yes, umm, ⁵____ , please.

Waitress Sure. Is that everything?

Jed Yes, thanks.

Waitress That's ⁶____ .

Jed Here you are.

Waitress That's ⁷____ change, thank you.

Lily Jed? What are you doing here?

Jed I'm having ⁸____ . I'm really hungry.

Lily But we're having a ⁹____ in the park in an hour!

Jed Don't worry. I can easily eat ¹⁰____ .

Lily Well, I want to see that!

▶ **Workbook** page 25, exercises 6–7

c Now role-play café conversations with your partner.

Can I help you?   Yes, please. Can I have..., please?

EXTRA Imagine you are vegetarian/very hungry/don't eat anything made with milk. Make more dialogues with your partner.

3B Going shopping

YOU FIRST! Do you help with the shopping for your family? Why? / Why not?

Vocabulary Quantities

1 a Look at the picture. What food and drink can you see?

b Match the correct words from the box with the food and drink in the picture.

> a bag   a bar   a bowl   a box   a can   a carton
> a cup   a glass   a kilo   a loaf   a packet   a plate
> a pot   a slice   a tin

c 🔊 **2.06** Listen and check. Practise saying the words.

d Test a partner. Your partner covers exercise 1b. Take turns pointing to something in the picture. Your partner says what it is.

2 🔊 **2.07** Listen. What does each person get?

3 a Draw a table. Put six things from exercise 1 on your table. Do not show your partner.

b Now ask and answer Yes / No questions with your partner. The first person to guess all of the things on their partner's table is the winner.

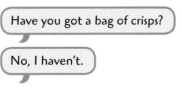

Have you got a bag of crisps?

No, I haven't.

Yes, I have. Have you got a plate of sandwiches?

c Compare your table with your partner's. Have you got any of the same things?

> ▶ **Workbook** page 26, exercises 1–3

Grammar *some* and *any*

4 a 🔊 **2.08** **Read and listen to the dialogue. What do they want to make?**

Elsa OK, what's in the recipe? First, ice cream and milk. There's some ice cream in the freezer, but there isn't any milk.

Lily OK. Let's buy some.

Elsa One carton or two?

Lily One carton, I think.

Elsa And are there any bananas at your house?

Lily A couple. We probably need some more.

Elsa OK. What else do we need? Do we need any cocoa powder?

Lily Yes, a small tin. Is that everything?

Elsa No, we need some straws!

Lily Oh, good idea!

b Which highlighted nouns are countable and which are uncountable?

c Find the words *some* and *any* in the dialogue. Then complete the rules with *some* and *any*. Find examples from the dialogue.

☞ **some and any**

We use *some* and *any* with countable nouns in the plural and with uncountable nouns.

☞ We use *some/any* with positive sentences, e.g. ____

We use *some/any* with…

- negative sentences, e.g. ____
- questions, e.g. ____

▶ **Workbook** page 27, exercise 4

Listening

5 🔊 **2.09** **Listen. What are the girls making? Why? Is it successful?**

6 a Complete the sentences with *some* or *any*.

1 We're making ____ banana milkshake.
2 Is there ____ milkshake for me?
3 We need ____ banana pieces first.
4 Then, pour in ____ milk.
5 Have you got ____ ice cream?
6 I didn't spill ____ of it.
7 Here's ____ milkshake for everyone.

b 🔊 **2.09** **Listen again and check your sentences.**

▶ **Workbook** page 27, exercises 5–6

Speaking

7 a Get ready to speak Go shopping! Look at the picture. What can you see?

b Look at your shopping list. Decide the quantities you need.
Student A Go to page 86. **Student B** Go to page 87.

c One person is the shopkeeper. Use the picture. Role-play the dialogue in the shop. Take turns being the shopkeeper.

Good morning. How can I help?

Hello. Have you got any water?

Yes, I have.

Can I have three bottles, please? Thank you. Have you got any milk?

No, I haven't got any milk, but I've got some juice.

No, thanks. I needed some milk for tea. Have you got any…?

 Work with a partner. Plan your dream party. What food do you need?

What did you have for breakfast this morning? Compare with a partner.

Reading and Listening

1 a What can you see in the photos?

a

b

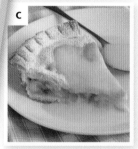
c

d

b Read the quiz and match the photos (a–d) to the correct questions.

c Ask and answer the quiz questions in pairs. Choose the answer nearest to your daily habits.

2 a Look at the scores at the end of the quiz and count up your total. Tick the box that shows the amount you scored.

b 🔊 **2.10** Listen to the explanation for your score. Do you agree with the advice?

c Compare with your partner's quiz score. Compare results with the class. Who are the healthiest people in the class?

Healthy Eating Quiz

Do you know how to eat healthily?
Or could you improve?
Find out by doing this quiz.

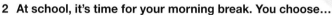

1 You are late for school and it's breakfast time. You…
A skip breakfast – you regularly do.
B have some sliced banana on cereal with milk and eat it before you go.
C make two slices of white toast and eat them on the way.

2 At school, it's time for your morning break. You choose…
A a cup of tea or fruit juice and two wholegrain biscuits.
B a can of cola and a chocolate bar.
C a glass of water and an apple.

3 How many portions of fruit and vegetables do you eat a day?
A A lot – 6 or more.
B Some – between 3 and 5.
C Not many – less than 2.

4 When you get a drink, what do you usually buy?
A A juice drink.
B A bottle of water, a smoothie or some fresh juice.
C A fizzy soft drink, like cola.

5 You're having lunch in a café. What do you choose?
A Grilled fish, potatoes and green salad.
B A ham sandwich, coffee and cake.
C A chicken pizza with tomatoes.

6 What do you usually prefer when choosing a dessert?
A Some home-made apple pie with custard.
B Some fresh fruit salad with yoghurt.
C A slice of chocolate cake with ice cream.

7 How much water do you drink a day?
A A lot – 5 to 10 glasses.
B Some – 3 to 5 glasses.
C Not much – 0 to 2 glasses.

8 How many sugary snacks do you eat a day?
A A lot. I like chocolate, sweets and ice cream.
B Some – I like them, but I don't always choose them.
C Not many – I try not to eat them most of the time.

Scores

8 a 0 b 1 c 2
7 a 2 b 1 c 0
6 a 1 b 2 c 0
5 a 2 c 0 c 1
4 a 1 b 2 c 0
3 a 2 b 1 c 0
2 a 1 b 0 c 2
1 a 0 b 2 c 1

0–7 ☐
8–12 ☐
13–16 ☐

Grammar *How much...? / How many...?;*
a lot (of) / not much / not many

3 a Complete these questions from the quiz.

____ water do you drink a day?

____ sugary snacks do you eat a day?

b Complete the rules with *How much...?,*
How many...?, a lot of, and *not much, not many.*

☞ We use ____ to ask about uncountable things.

We use ____ to ask about countable things.

We use ____ to talk about both uncountable and countable quantities.

We use ____ to talk about small countable quantities.

We use ____ to talk about small uncountable quantities.

4 Complete the questions with *How much...?* or *How many...?* Then ask and answer the questions with a partner. Use these words to reply.

A lot.   Some.   Not much. / Not many.

1 ____ sweets do you have a day?
2 ____ cans of fizzy drink do you have a day?
3 ____ fruit do you eat a day?
4 ____ bags of crisps do you eat a week?
5 ____ fish do you eat a week?
6 ____ meat do you eat a week?

▶ **Workbook** page 28, exercises 1–4

Listening

5 a 🔊 **2.11** Look at the topics in the box. Listen to the interview. Number the topics in the order that you hear them.

breakfast dessert dinner drinks lunch snacks

b 🔊 **2.11** Listen again and take notes.

Yesterday

Breakfast

Lunch

Dinner

Drinks

Snacks

c What do you think of Mia's diet? Can she improve it? Discuss with a partner, then tell the class.

Mia's diet is quite... She eats... She needs to...

▶ **Workbook** page 29, exercise 5

Speaking and Writing

6 a Get ready to speak Write a food diary for yesterday.

b Ask and answer questions about your diary with a partner. Make notes about your partner's diary.

What did you have for breakfast?

Toast and butter.

How many slices of toast did you have?

Two slices.

c Who was the healthiest yesterday?

7 a Get ready to write Write your partner's food diary using your notes from exercise 6.

Breakfast	two slices of toast and butter
Lunch	
Dinner	
Drinks	
Snacks	

▶ **Workbook** page 29, exercise 6

b Now write a short summary about your partner's diet. What does he / she do well? Can he / she improve it?

Ali's diet is... He eats... but he doesn't eat... He needs to...

EXTRA Imagine the food diary of a very healthy sportsperson. What do they eat and drink? Work with a partner to write the sportsperson's food diary for one day.

YOU FIRST! Where's your favourite place to eat? Home? At a relative's house? At your favourite restaurant? Why?

1 a ◍ 2.12 ▶ Read and listen.

Jed Hey Lily! Elsa! Listen. I wanted to do something Australian for you guys.

Lily That sounds good. What?

Jed A barbie.

Lily A what?

Jed A barbecue! You know – cooking outside and all that. Some nice food, some music…

Elsa Sounds good! Can you cook?

Jed Elsa, every Aussie knows how to do a barbecue. Come at lunchtime on Saturday.

Elsa The weather forecast isn't very good.

Jed Weather forecasts! What do they know?

1

2 Saturday

Jed's dad	Here. Give me your umbrellas.
Lily	Thank you. And here's some potato salad.
Jed's dad	That's very kind. Could you take it to the kitchen, please? Jed is barbecuing there.
Elsa	Can you barbecue inside?
Jed's dad	I guess you can!
Lily	Wow!
Elsa	This looks amazing.
Jed	Welcome! Aussie barbecue – English style!

Jed's mum	Hi girls! Jed, could you get drinks for Elsa and Lily?
Jed	No problem! Two special cocktails on their way!
Jed's mum	Is Alfie coming?
Lily	Yes, he is. He went home to get something first. What are we having?
Jed	Lamb burgers and snags coming up!
Elsa	Snags?
Jed	It's an Aussie word for sausages! Now, put some of everything on your plates!
Lily	Happy to. I'm very impressed.
Alfie	Hey, don't laugh. I thought: the weather is English, but I can dress Australian.

3

b Are the sentences true (T) or false (F)?

Jed invites his friends for dinner.

The weather is nice.

ed is barbecuing in the garden.

lfie is dressed like an Australian.

2 a Spoken English **What do these expressions mean? How do you say them in your own language?**

Like what?	A what?	…and all that.	Sounds good!	What do they know?

b Work in a group. Practise the dialogues.

▶ **Workbook** page 30, exercise 1

t 3 • **Food and health**

3 **a** What do Jed and his parents think of Alfie's outfit?

b 🔊 **2.13** ▶ Now listen and check your ideas.

4 **Over to you!** Work with a partner. Answer the questions.

1 What do you think of Jed's barbecue?
2 Do people in your country like eating outside?
3 How often do you have picnics or barbecues?

Everyday English

Giving instructions and polite requests

5 **a** Look at the useful phrases. Find examples in the dialogue in exercise 1.

Giving instructions – Imperatives

Come at lunchtime on Saturday.   Don't laugh!

Polite requests

Can you…?

Could you…, please?

Agreeing

Happy to.

No problem.

Refusing

No, I can't. I'm sorry.   Sorry, I can't at the moment.

b 🔊 **2.14** Listen and repeat.

▶ **Workbook** page 30–31, exercise 2

Pronunciation /ɑː/ /æ/

6 **a** 🔊 **2.15** Listen and repeat the words. Put them in the correct columns.

and   are   ask   barbie   can
can't   fantastic   grab   hard
having   lamb   snag   starting

/ɑː/	/æ/
are	and

b 🔊 **2.16** Listen and check.

c Say these words. Is it /ɑː/ or /æ/?

ankle   ant   arm   attic   aunt   bath
dance   dark   family   guitar   lamp
map   moustache   stand   start

▶ **Workbook** page 31, exercise 3

Listening and Speaking

7 **a** 🔊 **2.17** Listen to three conversations. What are the people asking others to do?

People	Request	Result
Dad and Tom	Hold this	Ok
Issy and Ali	Give too bag	ok you can lend it
Joe and Ella	Hw b/q	

b 🔊 **2.17** Listen again. What were the instructions? Can you remember any? Check with a partner.

▶ **Workbook** page 31, exercises 4–5

8 **a** Get ready to speak Look at the requests. How do you make them polite?

1 come to my party
2 lend me some money
3 let me use your computer
4 help me wash the car
5 show me your homework
6 carry some shopping for me

b Role-play with a partner. Use the prompts from 8a and take turns making polite requests. Use this chart to help you:

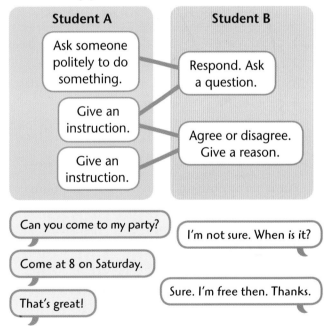

Student A	Student B
Ask someone politely to do something.	Respond. Ask a question.
Give an instruction.	Agree or disagree. Give a reason.
Give an instruction.	

Can you come to my party?

I'm not sure. When is it?

Come at 8 on Saturday.

Sure. I'm free then. Thanks.

That's great!

c Role-play one of your dialogues for the class.

 Invite your partner to a birthday party. Tell them what food you are making. Your partner asks questions.

Can you come to my birthday party?

Sounds great, thanks. What are you…?

I'm making some…

Unit 3 · Food and health

3 Revision

Vocabulary Food and drink nouns

1 Look at the pictures. Write the words.

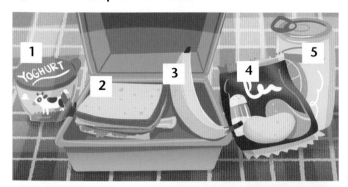

Quantities

2 Complete the sentences with the words in the box.

> kilo box carton cup packet pot slice

1 Could I have a ____ of tea and a ____ of cake, please?
2 Is that your ____ of sweets?
3 I sometimes have a ____ of yoghurt for breakfast.
4 Could I have a ____ of green apples, please?
5 Can you buy a ____ of milk and a ____ of eggs, please?

Grammar Countable / uncountable nouns

3 Put *a, an* or nothing (–) in front of the nouns.

1 Do you like ____ chocolate?
2 Would you like ____ apple or ____ banana?
3 I don't like ____ grapes.
4 I always have ____ cheese sandwich for lunch.
5 I never drink ____ coffee. I don't like it.

some and *any*

4 Complete the dialogue with *some* and *any*.

A There isn't ¹____ butter in the fridge.
B OK. I can buy ²____ at the shops later. Do we need ³____ milk?
No, but we didn't buy ⁴____ bread yesterday.
OK. And I'll get ⁵____ apples. Do we need ⁶____ vegetables?
es, get ⁷____ carrots, please.

How much...? / How many...?

5 Write the questions.

1 We've got some eggs. <u>How many eggs have we got</u> ?
2 She eats a lot of sweets. ____ ?
3 We need some chicken. ____ ?
4 They've got some bottles of lemonade. ____ ?
5 I drink a carton of milk every day. ____ ?

Everyday English

Giving instructions and polite requests

6 Complete the dialogue with the words in the box.

> ~~can you~~ could you find it
> happy problem sure

A <u>Can you</u> give me my tablet back?
B ¹____ to. I just need to find it.
A You've lost it? ²____ now, please.
B No ³____ . And it isn't lost. I just don't know where it is in my room.
A ⁴____ hurry up, please?
B ⁵____ . Phew, here it is.

Learning to learn
How do you remember words?

7 Look at these ways of remembering words and discuss them with a partner. Which do you do? Which do you not do? Which could you try to do in future?

1 Labelling pictures, e.g.
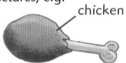

2 Listing word families,
e.g. to cook [v]
– a cook [n person]
– a cooker [n thing]

3 Drawing spidergrams e.g.
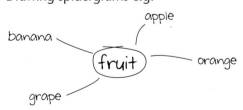

4 Making a topic list, e.g. Going shopping: Can I have...? Is there any...? Have you got any...?

5 Writing your own dictionary, e.g. lamb [n] a type of meat, from a baby sheep

▶ **Workbook** pages 32–33, exercises 1–7

3 · Food and health

My project

YOU FIRST! Do you have a healthy life? What do you do that is good? What do you do that is not so good?

six tips for healthy living

Eat Some FISH
GO TO BED EARLY
RUN or WALK for 30 minutes

1 Find a large piece of paper. Cut it into a shape like this.

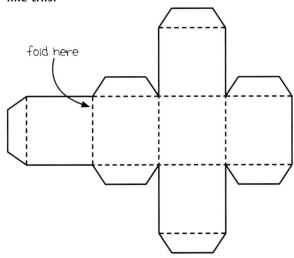

fold here

2 Look at the cube above. Are the tips for diet or staying active? Match the tips and pictures.

3 a Think of some healthy living tips: three tips for eating well and three tips for staying active.

b Write instructions on your cube for healthy living.
Walk to school today!

c Find some photos or draw some pictures on each side of your cube.

4 a Now put your cube together.

b With a partner, roll your cubes. Compare the instructions. Choose the best one. Do it today!

c Use your cube. Roll it once every day for a week. Do what it says each day. Report back to class.

3 Culture

YOU FIRST!

Do you like cooking or watching cooking programmes? Why? / Why not?

HEALTH HERO

JAMIE OLIVER

1 Jamie Oliver has a lot of energy – he is a chef, cookbook writer, and a TV food and health activist, as well as a father of five children. He wants everybody to eat well and live well, especially children. He was born north of London in Essex in 1975 and made his first TV programme at the age of 23. His relaxed, friendly style makes him very popular. In 2003, the Queen gave him an award for his contribution to the British food industry.

2 He regularly makes TV programmes and documentaries about food and society. He hates junk food and worries about children's health. In his TV programme *Jamie's School Dinners*, he worked in schools to try to make better lunches for pupils. He only used fresh food and taught the school cooks some healthy recipes. After the programme, the British government decided to improve school meals.

3 Jamie is dyslexic and can't read very well, so he had some problems at school and left at 16. But fortunately he loved cooking, so he studied to become a chef. He wanted to help young people. He believed that schools didn't help students who have problems. So he made a TV programme called *Jamie's Dream School* and tried to teach students who weren't doing well. He helped a lot of young people.

1 a Look at the photos. What do you learn about the person? Read paragraph 1 and answer the questions.

1 When and where was he born?

2 What is his job?

3 How many children has he got?

4 When did he first appear on TV?

5 What did he get an award for?

b Work with a partner.

Student A Read paragraph 2 about Jamie's TV cooking programme.

Student B Read paragraph 3 about Jamie's TV school programme.

Remember the information. Tell your partner. Do not look at your book!

c Discuss the questions.

1 What was the most interesting fact in each paragraph?

2 Why do you think Jamie does all of these things?

2 Over to you! Are there any famous TV chefs in your country? Are there any popular health programmes? Do you watch them? Why? / Why not?

 Healthy food

What sports do you watch / play?
Do you like sports? Why? / Why not?

Some steps to keep you healthy!

A Apps that count the number of steps you take are very popular. Experts say young people need to walk ¹____ steps a day to keep healthy. The average adult only walks around ²____ steps a day, but many teenagers play sports, so they take many more steps.

B However, the average teen can also spend over ³____ a day on various media, including watching TV, surfing online, and playing video games. And they also study hard for exams.

C So, how much exercise do you get? 10,000 steps are the same as ⁴____. It only takes about ⁵____ to walk 100 steps. So, in 30 minutes, young teens can take about 3,300 steps. How many steps do you take each day?

D And look at the time you spend on exercise. Teenagers need ⁶____ a day – some aerobic exercise for a healthy heart and some strength training ⁷____ for strong muscles and bones. This includes running, jumping and skipping.

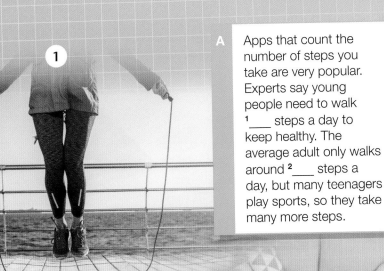

1 Look at the photos. What can you see?

2 a Read the paragraphs (A–D) and match them to the photos (1–4).

b Put the numbers in the correct places.

> 3,000–4,000   12,000   eight kilometres
> one hour   one minute   seven hours
> two or three times a week

c 🔊 **2.18** Listen and check.

3 Over to you! What do you think? Discuss with your partner.

1 How much exercise do you get a week? How many hours? Work out an average.

2 Can you work out approximately how many steps you take a day?

3 Compare with the class. Who takes the most steps?

4 a 🔊 **2.19** Listen to Orin talking about his ideal exercise plan for the week. Copy and complete the timetable.

Monday	PE for 1 hour
Tuesday	
Wednesday	
Thursday	
Friday	
Saturday	
Sunday	

b Write your ideal exercise plan for the next week. Try to stick to it!

c Report back to the class at the end of the week.

4 High-tech

4A Online

How often do you use the internet? What do you use it for? Compare with a partner, then discuss as a class.

Vocabulary The internet and computers

1 a Match the words in the box to the photos.

> camera   charger   games console
> keyboard   laptop   printer and scanner
> touchscreen   wireless router

b 🔊 **2.21** Listen and repeat.

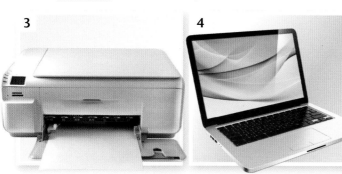

2 a Work with a partner. Match these words and definitions.

> download   go online   post   upload

Verbs

1 connect to the internet
2 take a file from the internet and put it on your computer
3 put a file from your computer on the internet
4 publish a message online

> blog   password   social
> media site   virus   vlog   Wi-fi

Nouns

5 a secret word that you use to open files
6 a hidden program that can break your computer
7 a journal you keep on the Web
8 a video diary you keep on the Web
9 a website where you can meet other people
10 a wireless connection to the internet

b 🔊 **2.22** Listen and check.

c 🔊 **2.23** Listen and repeat.

3 🔊 **2.24** Listen to three conversations and match the topics. There is one extra.

Conversation 1 _____ 2 _____ 3 _a_

a remembering passwords
b making a vlog
c looking at social media sites
d a possible virus

4 Work with a partner. Ask and answer the questions about your internet habits. Give more information.

What device do you use to go online?
Do you ever download music or movies?
Do you ever upload videos or photos?
How do you remember passwords?
Do you use any social networking sites?

> What do you use to go online?   Usually my phone.

➤ **Workbook** page 34, exercises 1–3

Grammar *will* for future

5 a Look at the two phones below. What do you think these phones can do?

b 🔊 **2.25** Read and listen to the web article. Is the Universal Internet a good idea? Why?/Why not?

The Universal Internet

Look at the first smartphone. Our technology changes fast, doesn't it? So, what will the internet be like in 15 or 20 years?

Experts agree that connectivity will become constant. In the future we won't use a password to go online because we will always be online.

The Universal Internet will become a reality: the things we own will talk to each other. Our houses, our cars, our fridges, our watches, even our own bodies, will be connected to the internet. Our lives will be completely connected, but perhaps they won't be any easier.

In this future world, will we have any privacy, any secrets? No, I don't think we will. I think that other people will see absolutely everything we do. Will that be a good thing? What do you think?

c Read the rules. Complete the examples from the text. Find one more example of each.

👉 We use *will* to make predictions about the future.
➕ We ___ always ___ online.
➖ We ___ ___ a password.
❓ ___ we ___ any privacy?
I think… will… is for personal predictions.

d What is *won't* short for?

6 a Complete the sentences with the correct form of *will*.

In the future…
1 all tablets ___ virtual keyboards. (have)
2 we ___ a charger for our computers. (not need)
3 ___ we ___ computer viruses all the time? (get)
4 students ___ to school. (not go)
5 students ___ online and do homework in chatrooms. (study)
6 everyone ___ blogs and vlogs to the internet. (upload)

b Discuss the ideas with a partner using *I (don't) think…will.*

> I think tablets will have virtual keyboards.

▶ **Workbook** page 35, exercise 4

Speaking and Listening

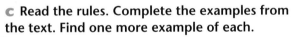

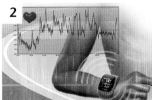

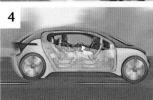

7 a Get ready to speak **Match the pictures with the topics in the box. What do you think they show?**

> factory production   farming   health   transport

b Work with a partner. What will these be like in the future? How will technology and the internet change things? Discuss ideas for each topic.

> I think that robots will work on farms in the future.

> I don't think they will.

▶ **Workbook** page 35, exercises 5–7

8 a 🔊 **2.26** Listen to the interview with an internet expert. Were your ideas in exercise 7b the same?

b 🔊 **2.26** Listen again and complete the sentences with the correct words from the listening.
1 Dr Paterson thinks that ___ cars will be much ___ .
2 We'll wear small ___ all the time and they'll ___ our ___ and tell us about any ___ .
3 We won't build big ___ any more. We'll use ___ to make the ___ we need.
4 We'll grow our food in vertical ___. We can use ___ to control the weather.

c What do you think of these ideas? Discuss with a partner.

> Dr Paterson thinks that people won't drive anymore. But I think that people like driving.

> Yes, but I think that people will…

 EXTRA Imagine your home in the future. Make predictions about what you think it will have. Tell a partner.

I think my house will be under the sea. It will have a…

YOU FIRST! How many gadgets have you used today?
Which is your favourite?

Vocabulary Technology / inventions

1 a Look at the photos and match the correct words from the box.

> 3D printer   driverless car   drone   e-reader   earphones   electric car
> games console   smartphone   smartwatch   virtual reality headset

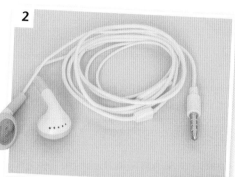

b 🔊 **2.27** Listen, check and repeat.

c Discuss the questions.

Which gadgets do you see in everyday life?
Which ones do you know how to use?

2 a 🔊 **2.28** Listen to four conversations.
Which invention are the people talking about?

1 ___   2 ___   3 ___   4 ___

b 🔊 **2.28** Listen again and answer.
Which invention…

1 …can fly?   3 …is quiet?
2 …isn't heavy?   4 …is tiny?

3 a Work with a partner. Choose your favourite
five inventions from exercise 1. Give your reasons.

b Write your top five technology items in order,
from most to least useful. Discuss with your partner.

> I think the most useful invention is…

> I don't agree. I think it's…

> OK. I don't mind. What do you think is number two?

c Now write the items in order of which you
would most like to have, from most to least
wanted. Are they in the same order?

▶ **Workbook** page 36, exercises 1–2

Reading and Grammar *be going to*

4 a Look at the photo. What's happening?

b Read the text about one person's invention. Would you like to try it?

Franky's Plan

Franky Zapata has got an amazing plan for us. In the future, humans are going to fly through the air. And we aren't going to need wings, just a small board. How are we going to do this? Well, Franky is the inventor of the Flyboard Air, and he holds the Guinness World Record for the longest distance on a travelling board. He's going to improve his design so that he can travel for longer. At the moment, the Flyboard Air isn't safe for everyone to use, but Franky and his team are going to improve safety so that anyone can fly on it.

c Read the rule and complete the examples from the text. Find two more examples.

☞ We use *be going to* to talk about future plans and intentions.

Positive

Humans ____ fly through the air.

Negative

We ____ need wings.

Question

How ____ we ____ do this?

5 a Look at the pictures and read the rule.

☞ We also use *be going to* for things we can see will happen.

b What is Franky going to do? Make sentences. Use these verbs.

crash   put on   fly

▶ **Workbook** page 37, exercises 3–4

Listening

6 a 🔊 **2.29** Listen. Match the gadgets to the teenagers.

Mia   Harry   Chrissie

electric car   smartwatch   VR headset

b 🔊 **2.29** Listen again and complete the table. Then tell the class.

	after school	future career	ambition
Mia			
Harry			
Chrissie			

After school, Mia's going to go to... She's going to be a...

▶ **Workbook** page 37, exercises 5–6

Speaking and Writing

7 a Get ready to speak **Complete the questions with *be going to* and the correct verb from the box. Write true answers.**

buy   do   live

1 What ____ you ____ when you leave school?
2 Where ____ you ____?
3 What ____ you ____ when you have enough money?

b Work with a partner. Ask and answer questions about your future.

What are you going to do when you leave school?

8 a Get ready to write **Make notes on your partner's answers from exercise 7a.**

b Write about your partner's future plans.

When ____ leaves school, he's / she's going to go to university. He's / She's going to study...

 EXTRA What are you going to do this evening / tomorrow / this weekend / this summer? Work with a partner. Tell them your plans.

4C Computer games

Do you like computer games?
If so, which ones? If not, why not?

BadTech is an evil organization that rules the world now. The boss of BadTech is called Malware. He uses a computer virus to control everybody through their laptops, smart phones and watches. Most of the people on the planet are now under remote control. They are called the Humanoids. Malware controls the Humanoids to hunt a secret group called the Freedom Guardians. He also uses special drones.

Your name is SmartTech. You are a Freedom Guardian. You are trying to get into Malware's top secret control room. Your mission is to find the main computer hard drive and destroy the virus. You need to:
- Look after the other Freedom Guardians.
- Get past the Humanoids. You can't touch them or you will become infected with the computer virus.
- Find Malware's secret headquarters within the main computer.

When you make a good decision, you will win lasers, secret information or medicine.

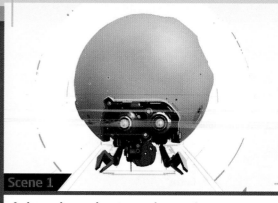

Scene 1

A drone is coming towards you. It can see your heartbeat. Your shield will hide your heart, but your friend hasn't got a shield. You can:

a escape from the drone to look for the secret door.

b try and rescue your friend.

Scene 2

A group of Humanoids is coming towards you. You:

a try and scare them with your new laser.

b run away, because the Humanoids mustn't touch you.

Scene 3

You're in Malware's control room. You:

a organize everyone and go straight for Malware.

b use the shields to move quietly and use the medicine to turn the Humanoids into Freedom Guardians

Reading and Listening

1 a Look at the video game pictures. What can you see?

b Read the story introduction. Discuss with a partner.

1 What is BadTech?

2 Who are these characters?

Malware   SmartTech   Humanoids   Freedom Guardians

3 What is your mission?

2 a Read the scenes. Choose a decision.

b 🔊 **2.30** Listen to the players. What do they decide? What happens? Compare your answers.

▶ **Workbook** pages 38–39, exercise 1

Grammar *will for decisions*

3 a Can you remember the decisions the players make? Can you complete them?

1 I ___ rescue you! I ___ run away.
2 I ___ stop them! I ___ let them touch us.
3 We ___ move forward slowly.

b 🔊 **2.30** Listen again and check.

c Look at the rule. Complete the examples from the dialogue.

☞ We often use *will* for immediate decisions,
e.g. Look out – a drone robot!
I ___ cover us both with a shield.
We can also use the negative.
We ___ make a noise.

4 Look at these situations. Think of a quick decision. What do you say? Use the verbs given.

> buy   go   invite   play tennis   ~~take~~

1 The dog wants to go out.
   I'll take the dog for a walk.
2 It's Mum's birthday next week.
3 There's no food in the fridge.
4 You want to play a video game, but not on your own.
5 It's raining and you want to stay in.

> **Workbook** page 39, exercises 2–3

Listening

5 a Look at the image from the video game. What can you see?

b 🔊 **2.31** Listen to the players playing more of the game. What's the twist in the story? Did you guess?

c What decisions do they make? Choose the correct ones.

1 I *'ll / won't* follow him.
2 I *'ll / won't* look.
3 I *'ll / won't* try the password.
4 We *'ll / won't* close the door.
5 We *'ll / won't* look for the control room.

d 🔊 **2.31** Listen again and check.

Speaking

6 a Get ready to speak Work with a partner. Look at your video game scenes. What can you see? Match the words and pictures.

> castle   desert   forest   lake
> mountain   jungle   sea   palace

Student A

CHOOSE YOUR PATH

Student B

CHOOSE YOUR PATH

b Take it in turns to decide which way you will take. Your partner will tell you what you will find. Which decision is the best / worst?

Student A Look at picture A, then go to page 86 to see what will happen to your partner.
Student B Look at picture B, then go to page 87 to see what will happen to your partner.

> I'll go through the forest.

> Then you will find a...!

EXTRA Write quick decisions for these situations.
You're hungry, bored, thirsty, tired.
I'll...

Are you good with computers and phones? Who do you ask when you don't know how to do something?

1 a 🔊 2.32 ▶ Read and listen. What does Jed talk about in his vlog?

Lily	Jed needs our help. He wants to make a vlog.
Alfie	Cool! You don't look very excited, Jed.
Jed	I don't like being in front of a camera, but it's for family and friends back home.
Elsa	Don't worry about that. Lily can do most of the talking.
Lily	Hey!
Jed	Do I need a camera?
Alfie	Your phone should be fine, but you should edit your videos before you upload them.
Lily	You should ask Elsa to edit them.
Jed	Elsa, can you do some editing?
Elsa	Sure, I'll help you with that.
Jed	Thanks, guys. That's really kind of you.

2 Later

Alfie	All set, everyone? And … action!
Jed	Hi everyone in Australia. Welcome to my vlog about my life on the opposite side of the world … the cold and rainy side.
Lily, Alfie, Elsa	Boo!
Jed	Now let me introduce my British friends. First, here's Lily.
Lily	Hi, everyone in Australia. How are you doing?
Jed	There's Alfie, who's filming me. And Elsa, who's editing these vlogs.

b Are the sentences true (T) or false (F)?

1 Jed is excited about his first vlog.
2 Jed offers to help his friends make a vlog.
3 Jed asks if Elsa can help him.

Jed	Now, I know you'll find this amazing, but my friends can't surf!

Jed	But they are really nice and very kind to me. Let's go and see where I live … Ow!
Lily	Let me help you with that.
Alfie	And … cut!

2 a Spoken English **What do these expressions mean? How do you say them in your own language?**

All set, everyone?   And … action!

And … cut!   Boo!

I know you'll find this amazing.

b Work in a group. Practise the dialogues.

▶ **Workbook** page 40, exercise 1

3 a Do you think Jed's vlog will be a success? Will other people like it?

b 🔊 2.33 ▶ Now listen and check your ideas.

4 Over to you! Work with a partner. Answer the questions.

1 Is Jed's vlog a good idea? Why?/Why not?
2 Do you vlog? Why?/Why not?
3 Do you watch vlogs on social media? Are they interesting?

Everyday English

Offering help

5 a Look at the useful phrases. Which examples below can you find in the story?

Offering help

Let me help you with (that)…   Can I help you?

Making helpful suggestions

Why don't you…   You should…

***Will* for offers**

I'll help you with that.   Sure we'll help.

Accepting help

That's great, thanks!   That's really kind of you.

b 🔊 2.34 Listen and repeat.

▶ **Workbook** page 40, exercises 2–4

Pronunciation The sounds /v/ /w/

6 a 🔊 2.35 Listen and repeat the words. Put them in the correct columns.

love   very   vlog   will   with   why

/v/	/w/
vlog	___
___	___

b 🔊 2.36 Listen again and check your answers.

▶ **Workbook** page 41, exercises 5–6

Listening and Speaking

7 a 🔊 2.37 Listen to three conversations. What are people offering to help with? Complete the first column of the table.

	What is the offer of help?	How does he/she help?
1		
2		
3		

b 🔊 2.37 Listen again. How do they help? Complete the second column of the table.

c Work with a partner. Compare your answers.

▶ **Workbook** page 41, exercises 7–8

8 a Get ready to speak Offer to help or make suggestions for three of these situations.

1 make dinner
2 look for someone's phone
3 fix someone's computer
4 a lift to school
5 upload a video
6 help someone with their homework

b Role-play. Work with a partner. Try different expressions. Use this chart to help you:

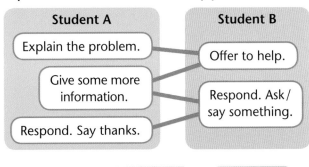

Student A	Student B
Explain the problem.	Offer to help.
Give some more information.	Respond. Ask/say something.
Respond. Say thanks.	

This homework is really difficult!   I'll help you.

Really? Thanks. I can't understand this geography…

Why don't you ask your teachers? They can help you.

OK. I will speak to them tomorrow. Thanks!

c Role-play one of your dialogues for the class.

 EXTRA Role-play. Work with a partner. Jed can't find something. Offer to help him. What is he looking for? Write the conversation.

Jed I can't find my phone!

You It's OK, I'll help you. Where…?

Vocabulary The internet and computers

1 Look at the photos and write the words.

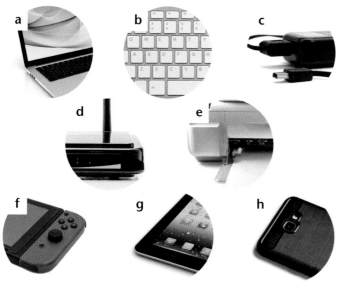

2 Choose the correct alternatives in the sentences.

1 *Go online / Upload* and see what the weather is like tomorrow.
2 I *post / download* photos on social media every day.
3 I'm writing a *vlog / blog* about my hobbies.
4 I want to listen to this music. Can you *download / password* it for me, please?
5 I have a lot of friends on *social media sites / Wi-fi.*

Technology / inventions

3 Read the descriptions and write the gadgets.

1 An aircraft without a pilot, controlled from the ground. ___
2 A small computer that you wear on your wrist. ___
3 A gadget to play computer games on TV with. ___
4 A machine connected to a computer that can make objects. ___
5 Something you wear over your ears to listen to music. ___

Grammar will for future

4 Complete the sentences with *will* and the verbs in the box.

> become   not be   not drive   not play   watch

1 The weather's bad, so we ___ our match this afternoon.
2 Computers ___ even smaller in the future.
3 People ___ cars in the future.
4 She's going to visit relatives, so she ___ at your party on Saturday.
5 I've downloaded a great film so we ___ it tonight.

be going to

	Tues	Wed	Thurs	Fri	Sat
Dave's Diary	finish homework	play football	buy birthday present	go with friends to the cinema	no homewo – hurray

5 Look at Dave's diary. Complete the sentences about his plans for the week.

1 On Tuesday, he ___ his friends.
2 On Wednesday, he ___ football.
3 On Thursday, he ___ a present for his sister.
4 On Friday, he and his friends ___ to the cinema.
5 On Saturday, he ___ any homework.

will for decisions

6 Complete the dialogues with the verbs in the box in the correct forms.

> answer   close   make   walk

1 'It's cold in here.' 'I ___ the window.'
2 'There's no bus this morning.' 'We ___ to school.'
3 'The phone's ringing.' 'I ___ it.'
4 'We're hungry.' 'I ___ some sandwiches.'

Everyday English

Offering help

7 Complete the dialogue with the words in the box.

> I can't   I'll help   problem   really kind   Why don't you

A ___ finish my homework. It's too difficult.
B ___ tell me what the ___ is?
A I don't understand this question.
B ___ you with that.
A Thanks, that's ___ of you.

Learning to learn
How do you search on the internet?

8 Look at this list and discuss them with a partner. Which do you already do? Which will you try?

- Use quotes ('') to look for an exact phrase, e.g. 'best films of 2019'.
- Use an asterisk (*) for words you can't remember in a phrase, e.g. as cold as *.
- Use 'vs.' to compare information on two types of foods, e.g. burger vs. pizza.
- Use define: to learn the meaning of words, e.g. define: wizard.
- Use the base word, e.g. bird, not birds.

> ▶ **Workbook** pages 42–43, exercises 1–8

YOU FIRST! Do you know any inventions that aren't useful? How could you make them better?

My invention

Business Plan
by James, Sara and Alex

NEW PRODUCT

We are going to make a new kind of bicycle helmet. It will be a folding helmet.

PURPOSE

This helmet is going to be for people who don't usually wear helmets. It will keep more people safe. A lot of people don't wear a helmet because they are difficult to carry during the day. Our folding helmet will fit into a bag easily!

PRODUCT DESIGN

The helmet is going to be made of plastic. It will shine in the dark. It will fit everybody.

FUTURE PREDICTION

More people are cycling to school and work. So everybody will want to have one.

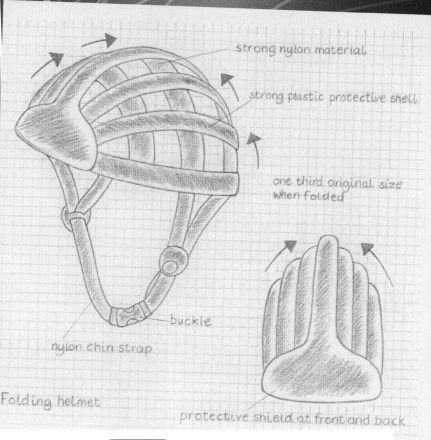

strong nylon material

strong plastic protective shell

one third original size when folded

buckle

nylon chin strap

Folding helmet

protective shield at front and back

1 a Work in a group. You are inventors. What are you going to invent next? Choose an idea from the list below or use your own ideas.

> A flying toothbrush that you don't need to hold
> A skateboard with a solar-powered engine
> A classroom robot
> A personal drone
> A driverless car for children

b Discuss your invention. Answer these questions.

1 What are you going to make?
2 Who is it going to be for? Who is it not going to be for?
3 What things is it going to do? How will it be useful?
4 What is it going to look like? Draw a picture.
  Size? Colour? Made of?

2 a Look at the business plan above. What is the invention going to be? Do you think it will be useful?

b Look at the questions in exercise 1b. Which part of the plan answers which question?

Look!

We use *going to* to talk about plans and intentions. But we don't repeat *going to* all the time. We can use *will* as well as *going to* to show certainty about future intentions.

We are going to make a new kind of bicycle helmet. It will be a folding helmet.

Find two more examples in the business plan.

c Write your business plan. You can use these phrases to help you.

> a new kind of   for people who
>   will be made of

3 a Present your business plan to the class. Answer questions from the class.

> This is our business plan for a new...

b Which invention is the most useful? Which is the most fun? Vote as a class.

4 Culture

How will computers change in the next 20 years?

The story of the
computer

A computer is any machine that can be programmed with a set of instructions.

1837

In Britain, the first machine with a program was designed by Charles Babbage and his pupil Ada Lovelace. Charles wanted a machine to add up big numbers, but Ada realized that a computer program could do a lot more. She was the first computer programmer.

1935

British scientist Alan Turing read Ada's ideas and invented the design for modern computers, with different programs to do different things. The Hollywood film *The Imitation Game* is about his brilliant mind.

1940s

Scientists built early computers in England and Germany. They were the size of a room!

1971

Ted Hoff, at US company Intel, was the main inventor of the microprocessor, or 'microchip'. After that, computers got faster and smaller very quickly.

1981

US company IBM designed the first PC (personal computer) for the general public. Experts didn't believe that anybody wanted a computer at home. But in two years people bought thousands of them.

1990s – 2000s

Smartphones – phones with a computer program – arrived!

The future

Scientists think that computers will be tiny. They will be everywhere, in our environment, in our clothes, and they will even be inside us!

---

1 a Work with a partner.

Student A Read from 1837 to the 1940s.

Student B Read from 1971 to the future.

b Ask and answer the questions.

Student A Ask Student B these questions.

1 What did Ted Hoff do?
2 What happened after his invention?
3 What did the IBM company do?
4 What happened in the 2000s?
5 What is the future of computers?

Student B Ask Student A these questions.

1 What did Charles Babbage do in 1837?
2 What did Ada Lovelace realize?
3 Who was Alan Turing?
4 Who built the early computers?
5 What did the early computers look like?

c What was the most surprising fact that you learned?

2 Over to you! Do you know any other famous inventors to do with computers? Do you know any other great inventions? Tell your partner.

Colossus

YOU FIRST!

You use the internet every day, but how much do you know about it? Discuss as a class.

The internet

1 a Look at the text on the right. Read the first two paragraphs and check your ideas.

b Complete the paragraphs with the words in the boxes.

1
| computer language under the water |
| wireless connection |

2
| became the internet |
| everybody in the world two US scientists |

c Can you explain these things?

| broadband TCP/IP Wi-fi World Wide Web |

d Look at the pictures (a–f). Match the technologies to the pictures.

Technologies and services available over the internet include:

1 Webpages – opened with a browser
2 Apps – opened without a browser, usually on smartphones
3 Email
4 File sharing
5 Voice calls
6 Streaming audio and video

2 a Imagine you are helping an English friend to use the internet. Label the diagram with these words.

| internet service provider router the internet web browser |

1 What is the internet?

The internet is a global network of computers that any computer can join. It uses a special "protocol", a kind of ¹ ____ , to connect different networks of computers, so that they can all talk to each other.

The internet comes to us on wires running underground, overhead and ² ____ . It also comes to us on radio waves and through satellite connections. To connect to the internet, you can use a phone line, or any cable connection. You also need a modem or router, which connects your computer to the network. This type of connection is a broadband connection. If you use a wireless router, you can also connect through radio waves without using cables. This is called a ³ ____ or 'Wi-fi'.

2 How did it happen?

In the 1960s, the US Army wanted to link all of its computers on one network. It was called ARPANET.

Then, in the 1970s, ⁴ ____ , Robert Kahn and Vinton Cerf, tried to link more networks to ARPANET. They developed a system called 'TCP/IP'. Using this method, the army network ⁵ ____ we know today.

In 1990, in the UK, Tim Berners-Lee invented the World Wide Web. With this, ⁶ ____ could see and use the internet. All you needed was a web browser and a network connection.

b 🔊 **2.38** Listen to the conversation and check your answers.

c Who is Lucy helping? What instructions does she give? Can you remember them?

d Role-play. Work with a partner. Role-play a dialogue between you and your English friend. Take it in turns to explain how to connect a laptop to a wireless router.

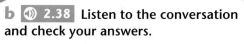

1 🔊 2.39 ▶ Read and listen to the story.

5A In the city

YOU FIRST! **What's your favourite city? Why? Describe it to your partner.**

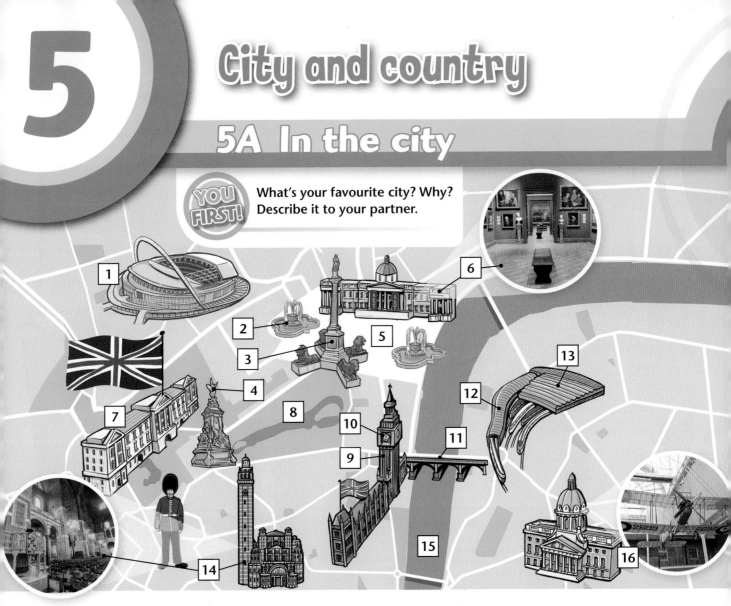

Vocabulary City places

1 a Look at the map. Which places in the city can you name?

b Match the words in the box with the places on the map.

art gallery bridge cathedral clock fountain
monument museum palace park river
square stadium station statue tower tunnel

c 🔊 3.02 Listen and check, then repeat.

2 Complete the table. Put the words from exercise 1 under the correct headings.

buildings and sights	open spaces	other
cathedral	square	bridge

3 a 🔊 3.03 Listen to the tour bus guide. Number the words in the table in exercise 2 in the order that you hear them.

b 🔊 3.03 Work with a partner. Compare your answers. Listen again and check.

4 a Work with a partner. Imagine an amazing city. Complete the text of a city tour guide with your own ideas. Include words from exercise 1. Use these phrases.

in front of you   in this street
look left / right and you can see

Good morning and welcome to the ¹___ city tour. We're starting our tour here in / at ²___. Look left and you can see ³___. Look right and you can see the famous ⁴___. Now, we're turning into ⁵___ Street where you can see the beautiful...

b Find a different partner. You are the tour guide. Role-play your city tour for your partner. He / She writes down the sights. Now listen to your partner's tour and write down the sights. Whose tour is more interesting?

Good morning and welcome to the ___ city tour. We're starting our tour here in the main square. Look left and you can see...

▶ **Workbook** page 46, exercises 1–3

Grammar Comparative adjectives

5 🔊 **3.04** **Read and listen.**
Which town does Jed prefer?

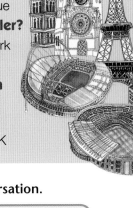

Lily   How does Oxford compare with your hometown?

Jed   Well, Oxford is much **older** than Mornington, and **bigger**, obviously.

Lily   Is Mornington beautiful?

Jed   It's beside the sea, which is great, but Oxford is **more beautiful**. It's **busier** here, though. I hate the traffic!

Lily   Yes, I'm sure Mornington isn't as busy as Oxford. But which do you prefer? Is Oxford **nicer** than Mornington?

Jed   It's difficult! I think Oxford is as nice as Mornington … but here the neighbours are **better**!

6 a **Complete the example, then complete the rule.**

Oxford is much ___ Mornington.

☞ We use a comparative adjective + ___ to compare two people, places, animals or objects.

b **Look at the highlighted adjectives in the dialogue. Copy and complete the table with examples.**

Comparative adjectives		
regular	near	nearer
short vowel and one consonant	big	
-e ending	nice	
-y ending	busy	
two or more syllables (not -y)	beautiful	
irregular	good	

c **Make the comparatives of these adjectives.**

famous   hilly   hot   interesting   tall   wide

(not) as...as...

7 a **Complete the sentence from the dialogue. Then answer the questions.**

Oxford is ___ Mornington.

1 Is Jed saying that both places are the same?

2 Can you find a negative form in the dialogue?

b **In pairs, give your opinion using *(not) as...as.***

1 cats / friendly / dogs

2 History / interesting / Geography

3 spring / nice / autumn

▶ **Workbook** page 47, exercises 4–6

Listening and Speaking

8 a **In pairs, do the city quiz. Guess if you do not know the answer.**

① **Which city is more ancient?**
   A Athens, Greece
   B Rome, Italy

② **Which city is more modern?**
   A San Francisco, USA
   B Tokyo, Japan

③ **Which city's clock is older?**
   A Big Ben, London
   B The Astronomical Clock, Prague

④ **Which city's monument is taller?**
   A Empire State Building, New York
   B Eiffel Tower, Paris

⑤ **Which city's football stadium is bigger?**
   A Camp Nou, Barcelona, Spain
   B Wembley Stadium, London, UK

b 🔊 **3.05** **Listen to the conversation. Check your answers.**

c **Make correct sentences using comparatives.**

> Athens is much older than Rome.

▶ **Workbook** page 47, exercise 7

9 a **Get ready to speak** **Look at the information.**

Mumbai	New York
over 20 million people	over 8 million people
started 1507	started 1626
32°C in summer	25°C in summer
20.5°C in winter	2°C in winter
Imperial Towers 256 m	One World Trade Centre 541 m

b **In pairs, ask and answer questions about the cities using these adjectives.**

beautiful   big   busy   cold
hot   interesting   old   tall

> Which city is bigger?

c **Write sentences comparing the cities.**

The One World Trade Centre in New York is taller than the Imperial Towers in Mumbai.

 EXTRA **Work with a partner. Compare two cities in your country.**

YOU FIRST! Do you prefer the city or the country? Why? Give reasons. Have a class vote.

Reading

1 a What can you see in the photos?

b Match the photos to the correct blog entry.

c Work with a partner. Complete the sentences.

1 Jen has got two…
2 She lives…
3 In summer she always…
4 One of her favourite things is…
5 To get to school she…
6 She and her brother don't like…

Living in **the wild**

Hello from the Hebrides!

A

1 20th May

Hi! I'm Jen and these are my brothers. Alec is 15 and is the oldest. Tom is the youngest.

We are ordinary teenagers. The most interesting thing about us is that we live on the Isle of Rum off the west coast of Scotland. It's wild here! Rum is the biggest island in the Inner Hebrides. But there are only about 30 people on it. There's only one shop, a tiny harbour, not many cars, and no mobile signal! But we can get the internet, so I'm writing this blog…

B

2 22nd July

It's the summer holidays. July and August are the hottest and nicest months of the year, but they are also the busiest. There is always work to do on the farm and the island, so everybody has more than one job. But the best thing is that my brothers and I have also got a lot of freedom. We go all over the island in any weather. I love watching dolphins from my kayak, riding my pony, and climbing the highest hills of the island where you get the most amazing view.

3 4th September

Alec and I are going back to school in Glasgow tomorrow. The worst thing is we have to travel by boat to the mainland with all our clothes and books. We are the students who live the furthest away from the school, so we need to stay there. We only come home once a month. We love school, but the most difficult thing is being away from our family. We can talk to everybody online, so it's OK.

According to a survey, the people living in the islands off Scotland are the happiest people in the UK. I agree. It's the best place in the world!

C

Grammar Superlative adjectives

2 a What is the most interesting thing you learned about Jen's life on Rum? Would you like to live there? Why?/Why not?

b Complete the example sentence. Then complete the rule.

> **Superlative adjectives**
>
> Rum is the ____ island in the Inner Hebrides.
>
> We use ____ + superlative adjective to compare a person, animal, place or thing with all of the group they are in.

c Copy and complete the table with examples. Check the text for the superlative adjectives.

Superlative adjectives		
regular	high	the highest
short vowel and one consonant	hot	
-e ending	nice	
-y ending	happy	
two or more syllables (not -y)	interesting	
irregular	far	

d Complete the examples from the text. Then complete the rules.

the old____   the young____

> To make superlatives we normally add -____ to the adjective.

the ____ amazing   the ____ difficult

> For adjectives with two syllables or more (not -y), we use ____ in front of the adjective.

What are the spelling rules for these adjectives?

big   busy   nice   good   bad

3 a Work with a partner. Make questions using superlative adjectives and ask and answer the questions. If you don't know – guess! Your teacher has the answers.

1 Which/cold/place/in the world?
2 Which/biggest/city/in the world?
3 Which/tall/building/in the world?
4 Which/small/country in the world?
5 Which/dangerous/animal/in the world?

b Write two more questions. Test your friends.

▶ **Workbook** page 48, exercises 1–3

Listening

4 a 🔊 **3.06** Listen to Jen and Magnus talking about the best place to live. Write J and/or M for each sentence.

1 ____ think(s) city life is best.
2 ____ think(s) city life is more interesting.
3 ____ think(s) country life is as exciting as city life.
4 ____ think(s) Glasgow is the best and friendliest city.
5 ____ think(s) Glasgow isn't as friendly as Rum.
6 ____ think(s) Rum is the best place for a holiday.

b What reasons do they give for their opinions?

c Who do you agree with most? Would you prefer a busier city life or a quieter country life?

Speaking and Writing

5 a Get ready to speak Make notes about the best place in the world for you.

1 Where is it? In the city or the country?
2 What does it look like? What has it got?
3 What is it best for? Write three things using superlatives.
4 Compare it to somewhere else using (not) as...as...
5 Why is it your favourite place?

b Work with a partner. Ask and answer questions about your place.

> Where is the best place in the world for you?

> It's Paris. Where is the best place for you?

> It's my grandparents' house!

▶ **Workbook** page 49, exercises 4–5

6 Get ready to write Use your notes from exercise 5a. Write about your favourite place.

> My favourite place is ____ .
> It's in ____ . It's got ____ . It's very ____ .
> It's the ____est place in the world, because ____ .
> It's got the ____ people. They ____ .
> It isn't as ____ as ____ , but I love it.

 EXTRA Work with a partner. Tell them your opinions on the best music, the nicest meal, the most exciting film, and the funniest TV programme.

Do you like reading maps? Do you use your phone for directions? Why?/Why not?

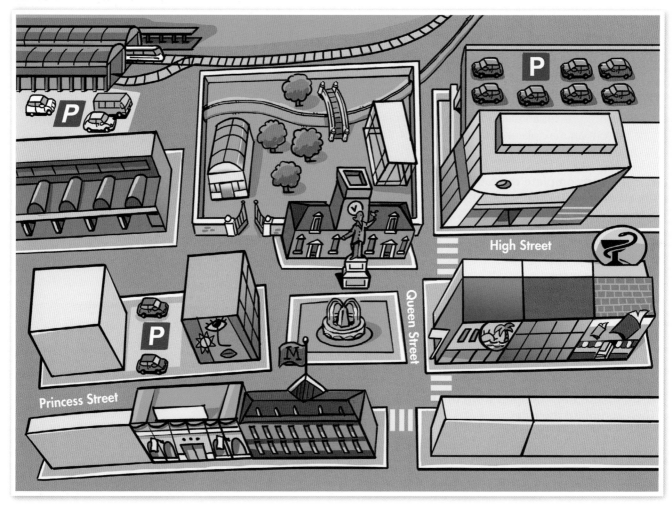

Vocabulary Prepositions of place

1 a Look at the street plan of a town centre. Complete the sentences with the words in the box.

> behind   between   in front of
> in the middle of   near   next to
> on the corner of   opposite   over   through

1 There's a fountain ____ the square.
2 There's a statue ____ the Town Hall.
3 There's a museum ____ the Town Hall.
4 There's a park ____ the Town Hall.
5 The river goes ____ the park.
6 The bridge goes ____ the river.
7 The train station is ____ the park.
8 The tourist office is ____ Queen Street and Princess Street.
9 There's a bus stop ____ the Tourist Office.
10 There's a car park ____ the train station and the bus station.

b 3.07 Listen and check, then repeat.

c Work with a partner. Test their memory. Your partner covers the picture. Ask questions with 'Where's...?'

> Where's the fountain?

> It's in the middle of the square.

2 3.08 Listen to the directions. Find the places on the map.

3 Decide where these places are on the map. Do not tell your partner. Ask and answer questions about the places.

> café   cinema   leisure centre
> newsagent's   sports shop

> Where's your café?

> It's in the middle of the park. Where's your café?

> My café is in the square.

➤ **Workbook** page 50, exercises 1–2

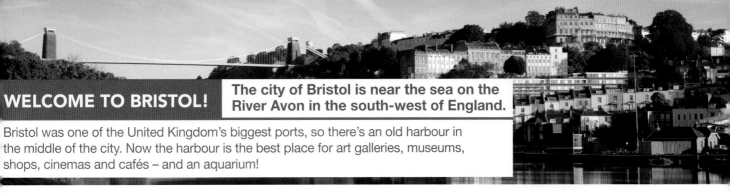

The official tourist guide VISIT BRISTOL!

WELCOME TO BRISTOL! The city of Bristol is near the sea on the River Avon in the south-west of England.

Bristol was one of the United Kingdom's biggest ports, so there's an old harbour in the middle of the city. Now the harbour is the best place for art galleries, museums, shops, cinemas and cafés – and an aquarium!

Grammar Definite and indefinite articles: *the, a / an*

4 a Read the tourist guide. What city places does it mention?

b Complete the sentences from the guide. Then complete the rules.

…there's ____ old harbour.
Now ____ harbour is the best place for shops.

👉 **1** We use ____ to talk about something for the first time.

2 We use ____ when we refer to something again. We know what it is.

3 We always use ____

- with positions, e.g. in the middle, on the left.
- when there is only one possibility, e.g. the south-west of England (there's only one).
- with superlative adjectives, e.g. the best.
- with countries using Republic, Kingdom, States, e.g. the United Kingdom.

5 a Complete Paul's email with *a, an, the* or nothing.

Dear Carlos,

My name's ¹____ Paul and I'm your exchange student. I'm looking forward to welcoming you to ²____ England!

Let me tell you about my home. I live in Bristol, ³____ city in ⁴____ south-west of England. We live in ⁵____ flat in ⁶____ Limerick Road. It's behind my school and about 25 minutes from ⁷____ centre of ⁸____ city.

There's ⁹____ old harbour in ¹⁰____ middle of ¹¹____ city. ¹²____ harbour is ¹³____ best area to visit. ¹⁴____ Aquarium and ¹⁵____ 3D Planetarium are there. They're fantastic places. I'll take you!

Paul

b 🔊 3.09 Listen and check.

c Read the email and answer the questions.

1 Do we use *the* with street names and people's names?

2 Do we use *the* with countries and cities?

3 Do we use *the* with rivers and well-known buildings?

➤ **Workbook** page 51, exercises 3–4

Listening and Speaking

6 a 🔊 3.10 Listen to two dialogues in a London tourist office. What do the students choose to do?

b 🔊 3.10 Listen again and complete the chart.

	Tourist attraction	Where?	Cost?
1			
2			

➤ **Workbook** page 51, exercises 5–6

7 a Get ready to speak Work with a partner. You work in the Bristol tourist office. Look at the information.

Student A Go to p86.   Student B Go to p87.

b Make dialogues at the tourist office. Ask these questions to get the information you need.

1 What exactly is it?   **4** How much is it?
2 What can I see there?   **5** Where is it?
3 When is it open?   **6** How do I get there?

Student A Answer your partner's questions about the Planetarium.

Student B Answer your partner's questions about the Aquarium.

> Good morning. How can I help you?

> Can I ask some questions about the Aquarium?

c Now use the information to compare the tourist attractions. Which is:

- cheaper?
- open longer?
- more interesting to you?

 EXTRA Work with a partner. Ask about these places. Describe where they are in your town.

a bank   the nearest bus station   a park
a supermarket   the Town Hall

5D A tour of the city

YOU FIRST! **Are you good or bad at following directions? Can you remember a time when you got some directions wrong?**

1 a 3.11 **Read and listen.**

1

Jed	Excuse me.
Passerby 1	Yes?
Jed	Could you tell me how to get to Lincoln College?
Passerby 1	I'm really sorry. I'm not from around here.
Jed	No problem. Thanks anyway… Excuse me, could you give me directions to Lincoln College?
Passerby 2	Certainly. Just go up this street and, at the top, turn right into the High Street. After about thirty metres, turn left into Turl Street. Go along Turl Street for about a hundred metres and Lincoln College is on your left.
Jed	That's great. Thanks a lot!
Passerby 2	You're welcome.

2 Later

Jed	Hi guys!
Alfie	Jed! You made it!
Jed	Yeah. Easy peasy. And I didn't use an app.
Lily	Here's your prize.
Jed	Awesome. I'm a proper tourist now!
Alfie	So what do you know about Oxford University?
Jed	It's old… very old.
Elsa	Excellent start.
Alfie	Give him a chance. Oxford is one of the oldest universities in the world. It started in 1096.
Jed	Wow! That is old.

3

Lily	Pay attention, Jed! That's just fact one.
Alfie	This is Lincoln College. It began in 1427.
Elsa	Fact two…
Jed	How many facts am I getting?
Alfie	Right, Jed. Last question for you. Which is the oldest university college?
Jed	I know this! It's a trick question. There are three very old colleges, but no one knows which one is the oldest.
Elsa	Not bad, Jed.
Jed	Thank you.

b Are the sentences true (T) or false (F)?

1 Jed knows the way to Lincoln College.
2 Jed is shopping in Oxford.
3 Alfie doesn't know a lot about Oxford.
4 Lily gives Jed a prize.

2 a Spoken English **What do these expressions mean? How do you say them in your own language?**

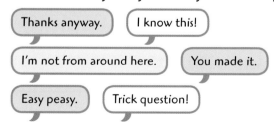

Thanks anyway.
I know this!
I'm not from around here.
You made it.
Easy peasy.
Trick question!

b Work in a group. Practise the dialogues.

➤ **Workbook** page 52, exercise 1

3 a Do you think Jed knows where the sights are in Oxford at the end of the tour? Does he pay attention?

b 🔊 **3.12** ▶ Now listen and check your ideas.

4 Over to you! Work with a partner. Answer the questions.

1 What did Jed learn on his tour of the city?

2 What's a trick question?

3 Have you ever shown a visitor around your town? Where did you go? What did they think?

Everyday English

Asking for and giving directions

5 a Look at the useful phrases. Which examples below can you find in the story?

Asking for directions

Excuse me, could you tell me how to get to…, please?

Excuse me, could you give me directions to…?

Excuse me, how do I find (the nearest)…?

Responding

No problem.   Certainly.

Thanks a lot.   You're welcome.

I'm really sorry. I'm not from around here.

Giving directions

Can you see that … over there?

Go up this street and, at the top,…

Turn left / right at the end of the road.

b 🔊 **3.13** Listen and repeat.

▶ **Workbook** page 52, exercise 2

Pronunciation Sounding polite

To sound polite, you start high and lift your voice again at the end for questions and requests. Generally use a wide voice range.

6 a 🔊 **3.14** Listen and repeat.

Excuse me?   Can I help you?

Could you tell me how to get to…

Lincoln College, please?

Certainly.

You're welcome.

b Work with a partner. Say the phrases in 6a and practise sounding polite.

c 🔊 **3.14** Listen again and repeat.

▶ **Workbook** page 52, exercise 3

7 a Match the directions (1–8) to the pictures (a–h).

1 go along the road until…   5 go straight ahead

2 go over the…   6 turn left

3 go past the…   7 turn right

4 take the second turning on the right   8 take the second turning on the left

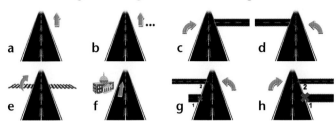

a   b   c   d

e   f   g   h

b 🔊 **3.15** Listen and check, then repeat.

▶ **Workbook** page 53, exercises 4–5

Listening and Speaking

8 🔊 **3.16** Listen to the directions. Look at the map on page 64. Where is each person going? Can you work out where they are starting from?

▶ **Workbook** page 53, exercises 4–5

9 a Get ready to speak Look at the map on page 64. Choose some different places to start from and to go to.

b Role-play with a partner. Ask for directions to the places. Try different expressions. Use this chart to help you:

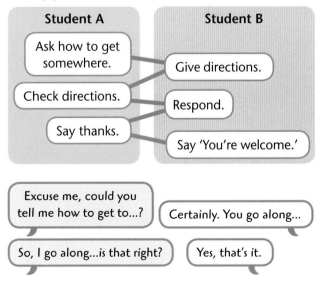

Student A	Student B
Ask how to get somewhere.	Give directions.
Check directions.	Respond.
Say thanks.	Say 'You're welcome.'

Excuse me, could you tell me how to get to…?   Certainly. You go along…

So, I go along…is that right?   Yes, that's it.

c Role-play one of your dialogues for the class.

EXTRA Direct your partner to a place from your classroom or from the school gate. Can your partner guess from the directions?

So, you go out of the school and turn left. You go along the road until you get to the corner…

Is it the park?

5 Revision

Vocabulary City places

1 Write the places.

1 ___   2 ___   3 ___

4 ___   5 ___   6 ___

Prepositions of place

2 Write the prepositions.

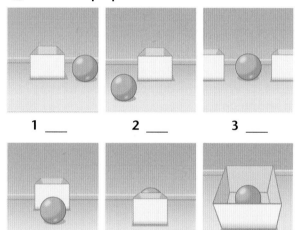

1 ___   2 ___   3 ___

4 ___   5 ___   6 ___

Directions

3 Write the directions.

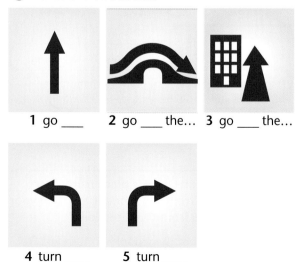

1 go ___   2 go ___ the...   3 go ___ the...

4 turn ___   5 turn ___

Grammar Comparative and superlative adjectives

4 Write the sentences, comparing two or more things.
1 My brother / short / me
2 Our dog / good / dog in the whole world
3 Maths / interesting / Science
4 Arturo / funny / boy in the class

(not) as...as...

5 Read each sentence. Complete the second sentence with *(not) as...as...* and the words in brackets so it has the same meaning as the first sentence.

1 Simon and Sam are the same height.   Simon...Sam. (tall)
2 Yesterday was windier than today.   Today...yesterday. (not windy)
3 Jen's phone is two years old and mine is, too.   My phone...Jen's. (old)
4 Gold is heavier than silver.   Silver...gold. (not heavy)

Definite and indefinite articles: *the, a / an*

6 Write *a, an, the* or nothing in the gaps.
1 I went to ___ Japanese restaurant. ___ restaurant was fantastic. It was on ___ Black Street on ___ corner.
2 ___ John travelled to ___ Mexico last month.
3 I'm going to ___ park in ___ centre of ___ city.
4 I finished ___ amazing book last night.

Everyday English

Asking for and giving directions

7 Complete the dialogue with the words in the box.

> certainly   excuse me   is that right   until   yes, that's it

A ¹___ , could you tell me how to get to the station?
B ²___ . You go along this road ³___ you come to a bridge. Turn left and it's at the end of that road.
A So, I go along this road in this direction, ⁴___ ?
B ⁵___ .
A Thank you very much.

Learning to learn Improving your speaking skills

8 Try these things to help your speaking.
1 Always try to speak English in class with your partner and the teacher.
2 When you are doing homework, read it out loud to yourself.
3 Find 'listen and repeat' exercises online.
4 In your everyday life, ask yourself, 'How could I say that in English?'
5 Don't worry about making mistakes!

➤ **Workbook** pages 54–55, exercises 1–9

My project

Imagine you have some exchange students coming to visit you. What are the best places to visit near you? Make a list.

A tour of your hometown

1 Kingsbridge is a small town in Devon in the south west of England.

Things to see and do:

- Take a boat trip along the wonderful Devon coast.
- Go shopping along Fore Street in the old part of town.
- Spend a day at one of the most beautiful beaches in Devon.
- Have the best Devon tea – scones, cream and jam!

2

Kingsbridge

Welcome to sunny Kingsbridge for a wonderful holiday in Devon!

3

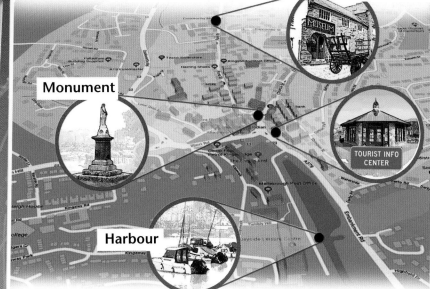

Museum

Monument

TOURIST INFO CENTER

Harbour

a Front page

b Inside

c Back page

---

1 a Work in small groups. Choose where you live (or a town or city you know well) and collect information about interesting things to do and see there.

b Find a large piece of paper. Fold it to make a leaflet. Design it like this:

Front page:

Name of place in colourful letters

Nice photograph with a caption

An inviting strapline, e.g. Welcome to sunny…! You'll have a wonderful time!

Inside:

Find or draw a simple map of the centre.

Highlight some of the important places.

Write a note for each place.

Back page:

Write sentences about the place.

Write a list of some things to see and do.

c Look at Ania's pieces of information (1–3). Which pages of her leaflet (a–c) should they go on?

2 a Put your leaflet together.

b Show your leaflet to the class. Discuss the questions.

1 Which is the most colourful?

2 Which is the most informative?

3 Which is the most helpful for a tourist?

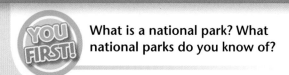

YOU FIRST! What is a national park? What national parks do you know of?

Two National Parks

Yellowstone, USA

Yellowstone became a park in 1872 and is the oldest national park in the world. It is huge – 8,983 km². A lot of the park sits in the middle of an active supervolcano, which is 72 km wide! It has four mountain ranges, and the highest mountain, Eagle Peak, is 3,466 m high. The park has 2,000,000 visitors every year.

What to see and do:

> Visit the volcanic hot springs and watch the geysers.
> Ride a horse or llama in summer or snowmobile in winter!
> Watch amazing wildlife: bears, wolves and bison.
> Go climbing, kayaking in the lakes, cycling or hiking. Explore!

Snowdonia, Wales, UK

It's Wales' oldest and largest national park. It became a park in 1951. It's 2,130 km² in size and it has nine mountain ranges. Mount Snowdon is 1,085 m high. It's a dead volcano and the highest mountain in England and Wales. The park is in one of the wettest parts of the UK, but that doesn't stop more than 3,000,000 visitors every year.

What to see and do:

> Climb to the top of Mount Snowdon for incredible views.
> Travel by horse in summer or mountain train in winter!
> Watch amazing wildlife: otters, eagles and polecats.
> Go climbing, kayaking along the rivers, cycling or hiking. Explore!

1 **a** Work with a partner. Decide who will read which fact file.

Student A Read about Yellowstone.

Student B Read about Snowdonia.

b Discuss the questions and compare the parks.

1 Which park is older?
2 Which park is bigger?
3 Which park has the higher mountain?
4 Which park has more visitors?
5 What is there to see and do?

c What was the most interesting fact in each text?

d Which park would you prefer to visit? Why?

2 Over to you! What are the most famous national parks in your country? What do tourists like to see and do there? Make a list.

The Grand Canyon

What do you know about these early civilizations?
Egyptian   Incan   Mayan

Sumer, Mesopotamia:
the world's earliest civilization

! FACT FILE

A 'civilization' means several cities with a shared culture, government, language, technology and writing.

A ___

The region of Mesopotamia began in Iraq. It had two ___ – the Euphrates and the Tigris – so it was very green. Mesopotamia means 'land between two rivers'.

B ___

Before 8000 BC, humans travelled around in small groups to look for food. But in 8000 BC people in Mesopotamia became some of the earliest farmers, because the land was so good. They started to live in the same place. Slowly, villages and ___ began to grow.

C ___

Around 4000 BC, Sumer in southern Mesopotamia had several ___ with governments. A written language called Sumerian began between the cities. Uruk was the largest city with about 680,000 people. It is considered to be the earliest city in the world.

D ___

The Mesopotamians invented new technology. They were the first to use the wheel in 3200 BC. They could ___ food anywhere. They also invented a number system based on 60 from 3000 BC. That's why we have 60 seconds in a minute and 60 minutes in an hour.

Sumerian – the language of ancient Sumer

The civilization of Sumer lasted for over 1,200 years.

1 **a** Look at the Fact file. Match the headings (1–4) to the relevant paragraphs (A–D).

 1 Why did it start?

 2 What did it achieve?

 3 When did it become a civilization?

 4 Where did it start?

 b Complete the text with these words.

 cities   rivers   towns   transport

 c 🔊 **3.17** Listen and check your answers.

2 **Complete the timeline. What happened at these times? There is one date on the timeline you do not need.**

9000	6000	3200
BC		0
8000	4000	3000

3 **a** 🔊 **3.18** What did the earliest cities look like? Listen to the description. Complete the diagram with the words in the box.

 city walls
 poorest homes
 royal palaces
 shops and offices
 ziggurat

 b 🔊 **3.18** What extra information can you remember? Listen again. Compare your ideas.

4 **Over to you!** What are the most famous historical sites in your country? Discuss with a partner.

A ziggurat in Iraq – rebuilt

6A Problems

 Who are the people you talk to when you have a problem? Why?

Vocabulary Phrasal verbs

1 a Look at the pictures. What can you see?

b Match each phrasal verb with its opposite. Then match them to the correct pictures.

> look at   look for   pick up   put down
> put on   sleep in   switch off   switch on
> take off   turn down   turn up   wake up

c 🔊 **3.20** Listen, check and repeat.

2 🔊 **3.21** 📝 Listen to three conversations. What are the problems? Do you ever have these problems? When? Tell a partner.

Look!

If we use an object pronoun, it goes between the two parts of the phrasal verb:

Pick up *the pen*.   →   Pick *it* up.

Take off *your gloves*.   →   Take *them* off.

3 a Work with a partner. Look at pictures 1–6. Read a line from A and your partner answers with the correct response. Take turns.

A	B
1 It's hot in here.	**a** Wow! Can I look at it?
2 I had a busy week and I'm tired.	**b** Turn on the fan.
3 It's so cold outside!	**c** I'll turn it up for you.
4 I have found a glass shoe!	**d** Put on your warm jacket.
5 We have a new pet spider for sale.	**e** Pick it up! It looks expensive!
6 I can't hear the music.	**f** It's the weekend. Sleep in!

b Look at pictures 1–6. Work with your partner to describe the situations and come up with appropriate responses. When you're finished, act out the dialogues for the class!

> This shoe smells bad!

> Quick! Put it down!

> ➤ **Workbook** page 56, exercise 1

Grammar *should / shouldn't*

4 a Read the online advice forum. What's Mark's problem? What's the best advice?

Teen Help Online

Mark   11/11 18.17 pm
Does anybody else have this problem? I have a lot of trouble getting up early in the morning for school. Does anybody have any advice or suggestions for me?

1 Liam   19.02 pm
You should switch on a bright light, play some lively music and turn up the volume. Then go and have a shower immediately. It's impossible not to feel awake after that.

2 Emmy   19.03 pm
I think Mark should go to bed early with a hot drink and switch off his mobile phone. He shouldn't stay up late. If he gets enough sleep he can wake up no problem.

3 Daisy   19.06 pm
It isn't your fault! Scientists say that all teenagers have this problem because they are growing, and that schools should start later. They say that teenagers shouldn't start to study until 10 or 11 o'clock.

b Complete the sentences from the dialogue in exercise 4a.

1 You ＿＿ switch on a bright light.

2 Teenagers ＿＿ start to study until 10 or 11 o'clock.

c What form of the verb do we use after *should*? Do we add *-s* with *he / she / it*?

5 When do we use *should / shouldn't*? Choose the correct answers.

☞ We use *should / shouldn't* to:

    a give advice.

    b check instructions.

    c make quick decisions.

6 Complete the advice using *should* or *shouldn't*. Work with a partner and practise the dialogues.

   1 I'm tired.
     You ＿＿ sit down and have a rest.
     You ＿＿ stay up late on your computer.

   2 I'm late for school.
     You ＿＿ wake up earlier.
     You ＿＿ switch off your alarm.

   3 I don't understand my homework.
     You ＿＿ work with the TV on. Switch it off.
     You ＿＿ ask someone for help.

> I'm tired.   You should sit down and have a rest.

> **Workbook** pages 56–57, exercises 2–3

Listening and Speaking

7 a 🔊 **3.22** Listen to the teen radio programme. What are the problems? Copy the table and make notes in the first column.

Problem	Advice

b 🔊 **3.22** Listen again. What advice does Tom give?

c What's your opinion on each piece of advice?

d Work with a partner. Choose one of the problems. Write some more advice for the person. Compare with the class.

> **Workbook** page 57, exercise 4

8 a Get ready to speak Read the problems and think of some advice. What would a friend say? What would an adult say?

   1 I'm hungry.

   2 I'm bored.

   3 I don't feel well.

   4 I'm a bit depressed.

   5 I don't like doing exercise.

   6 I had an argument with my friend yesterday.

b Work with a partner. Make dialogues giving advice. Use *should / shouldn't* and *I think you should / I don't think you should*.

> Mum, I'm hungry.

> You should have a snack. But you shouldn't eat too much. Dinner will be soon.

> Can I make a sandwich?

> I think you should have some fruit.

EXTRA What advice do adults give to teenagers? Discuss with a partner. Make sentences with *should / shouldn't*. How do you answer? Role-play the dialogues.

I feel tired.

You should go to bed earlier on schooldays.

Think of examples of rules at home / at school. Compare with a partner. Which rules are most important? Why?

Vocabulary Adverbs with -ly

1 a Look at the words in A and match them to their opposites in B. Which can you see in the pictures (a–f)?

A badly carelessly	**B** carefully happily
dangerously loudly	nicely quietly
quickly sadly	safely slowly

b ◀)) **3.23** Listen and check. Practise saying the words.

> **Look!**
>
> **1** We usually make adverbs by adding -ly to an adjective: *quick* → *quickly*
>
> **2** An adverb describes a verb. Look at the position of the adverb. It often goes at the end of the sentence.
>
> *The boy is cycling **quickly**.*

2 Write the sentences and match them to the pictures (a–f).

1 cycle / quick  – b
2 open present / happy
3 do Maths / careless
4 skate / bad
5 skateboard / dangerous
6 bang drum / loud

3 ◀)) **3.24** Listen. Choose the correct adverb to describe the action.

4 a Choose one of these actions. Then choose an adverb and mime the action in that way. Your partner guesses the action and the adverb.

> brush your teeth   cook something   drive a car
> play the guitar   say something   sit down on a chair
> switch on the TV   write something

Are you brushing your teeth carelessly?

Yes, I am.

b Play again. Choose your own actions.

▶ **Workbook** page 58, exercises 1–2

Grammar *must / mustn't*

5 a Where can you see these signs? Match the signs to the places.

> at a road crossing   at school   in a museum
> in a zoo   on a pavement   on a road

a   b

c   d

e   f

b Match the rules (1–6) to the signs (a–f).

1 You mustn't ride a bike here. ____

2 You mustn't feed the animals. ____

3 You must turn left here. ____

4 You mustn't pick up anything in here. ____

5 You must wait to cross the road. ____

6 You must switch off your mobile phone. ____

c Look at the example sentences. Complete the rules with *must* and *mustn't*.

You must turn left here.

You mustn't feed the animals.

☞ We use *must* and *mustn't* to talk about rules and to give strong advice.

We use ____ to say is a rule.

We use ____ to say it is against the rules.

d Complete the sentences with *must* or *mustn't*.

1 We ____ skateboard on the tennis courts.

2 You ____ cycle safely and wear a helmet.

3 You ____ run next to the swimming pool. You ____ walk slowly.

4 We ____ work quietly in an exam.

▶ **Workbook** page 58, exercise 3

Listening

6 a 🔊 **3.25** Listen to four conversations and match them to the signs. There are two signs you don't need.

a   b   c   d   e   f

b What do they say? Write the sentences.

1 talk / quiet   3 climb down / safe

2 play music / loud   4 throw rubbish away / careless

c 🔊 **3.25** Listen again and check.

d Work with a partner. Write sentences using *must / musn't* to explain the two extra signs.

Speaking and Writing

7 a Get ready to speak **Make some rules for each of these places.**

> a park   a playground   a shopping centre
> a swimming pool   a train station   library

b Work with a partner. Give your partner a rule for one of the places. Your partner guesses the place.

 You mustn't run around dangerously.   A playground?

▶ **Workbook** page 59, exercises 4–5

8 a Get ready to write **Work with a partner. Think of some new fun rules for school. Use these ideas:**

> birthdays   clothes   food   holidays
> things schools must give to students
> things teachers must do for students

b Complete the noticeboard with six or more new fun rules. Use *must* and *mustn't*. Show the class.

NEW SCHOOL RULES – FOR FUN!

❶ All students must wear bright colours.

❷ Teachers must allow picnics in the classroom.

❸

 Role-play. Work with a partner. Pretend you are your partner's parent! Give them some new rules.

YOU FIRST! Can you remember the last time you needed to make a difficult choice? What did you decide? Think and tell your partner.

Reading and Listening

1 a Look at the photos and answer the questions.

1 What can you see in the photos?

   a Losing money   **b** Finding money

2 What do you think the second story will involve?

   a Escaping from lions   **b** Saving some lions

b 🔊 **3.26** Read and listen to the real-life dilemmas and check your ideas.

c Imagine yourself in the situations. Choose a response. Then discuss with the class.

d Do you think the stories will have a happy ending? Why? / Why not?

2 a 🔊 **3.27** Now listen to the endings to the real-life stories and compare your ideas. What did each person decide to do?

b 🔊 **3.27** Listen again and answer the questions.

1 What did the Boston police do for Glen?

2 How did Ethan Whittington hear about Ben?

3 What did he do for Glen?

4 Why did the safari park workers want Helen and her children to stay in the car?

5 How did they get out of the lion enclosure?

3 Which story was the more surprising? Did you like the stories? Why? / Why not?

▶ **Workbook** pages 60–61, exercises 1–2

1

The story of Glen James

He was a homeless person who lived on the streets of Boston, USA, for over seven years. One day, he slowly walked into a shopping centre. It was warm and dry so he sat down. He saw a man with a rucksack. Later, he looked up – there was no man, but the rucksack was still there. He picked up the rucksack and opened it quickly, to see what was inside. He found over $2,000 in cash and $40,000 in traveller's cheques.

What do you think?

1 He doesn't have to give the bag to the police. He can keep it and stop living on the streets in the cold and wet. He can even help other homeless people with the money.

2 He has to take the bag to the police station. It isn't his and it isn't his money. It's wrong to take another person's money.

Real-life DILEMMAS

The story of Helen Clements

She was taking her children to Longleat Safari Park in the UK. It was a hot day and she was driving through the lion area. Then, her car caught fire. Smoke was coming into the car. She and her children couldn't breathe very well. She sounded the car horn, but no one came. She switched the engine off. The car could explode! The lions came to see what was happening. The children were crying.

What do you think?

1 She has to get out of the car with her children immediately. The burning car is much more dangerous. She has a better chance of survival with the lions.

2 She doesn't have to get out of the car. She can open the doors so the smoke goes out. She can't run away from lions with two children. It's better to wait for help.

Grammar *have to / don't have to*

4 a Complete these sentences from the reading.

1 He ___ the bag to the police.

2 He ___ the bag to the police station.

b Complete the rules with the correct option.

a *don't have to / doesn't have to*

b *have to / has to*

> We use ___ to say what is necessary to do.
>
> We use ___ to say what is not necessary to do.

c Find more examples of each form in the text.

5 Write the sentences. Use the correct form of *have to*.

1 Sam ___ finish his homework. He will be in trouble if he doesn't.

Sam has to finish his homework.

2 Sally ___ tidy her room. Her mum told her to.

3 They ___ go to school today. It's Sunday.

4 We ___ take the dog for a walk. It's one of my jobs.

5 Bob ___ wash the dishes. His family has a dishwasher.

6 I ___ go to bed early. My parents will be angry if I don't.

Look!

> You *mustn't* go out today. (It is forbidden.)
>
> You *don't have to* go out today. (You can if you want, but it isn't necessary.)

6 Rewrite the sentences using *mustn't / don't have to*.

1 Don't switch that on! It's dangerous.

You mustn't switch that on...

2 You can finish the exercise if you want to.

3 Don't get up. You're not well.

4 He doesn't need to turn down the music. I like it.

5 Shh! Be quiet in here!

7 Match the actions to the situations. Make two sentences using *mustn't* and three sentences using *don't have to*.

Actions
be rich
go to bed early
tell the secret
touch the animals
use a knife and fork

Situations
at the zoo
on Saturday night
to anyone
to eat pizza
to be happy

You don't have to use a knife and fork to eat pizza.

> **Workbook** page 61, exercises 3–5

Listening and Speaking

8 a 🔊 **3.28** Listen. Copy the table below and complete the gaps in Claire's diary. Choose from these words to help you:

> a match   Art club   dentist
> football   nothing to do   Grandma's
> swim training   training   visiting family

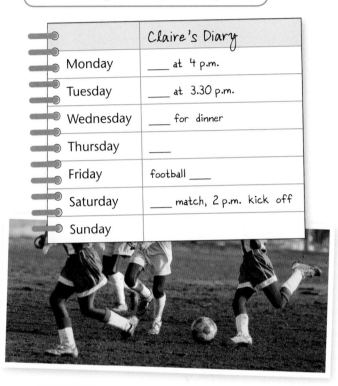

Claire's Diary

Monday	___ at 4 p.m.
Tuesday	___ at 3.30 p.m.
Wednesday	___ for dinner
Thursday	___
Friday	football ___
Saturday	___ match, 2 p.m. kick off
Sunday	

b 🔊 **3.28** Listen again and make a diary for Jake. When do they meet up?

9 a Get ready to speak Look at your diary for next week.

Student A Go to page 86.

Student B Go to page 87.

b Look at what you want to arrange with your partner. Ask and answer questions about your diary with your partner. What can you arrange for next week?

> What are you doing on Monday after school?

> I have to go to the dentist at 4.00. Why don't we get together after that?

> Hmm...I think that'll be difficult because I... What about...?

EXTRA Write down three things that:

1 you have to do during the week.

2 you don't have to do on Sundays.

Compare with a partner.

YOU FIRST! Are you good at trying new things? Why?/ Why not? What sort of things will you try out?

1 a 🔊 **3.29** ▶ Read and listen. What does Lily ask Jed to do?

Elsa Do you like living here now, Jed?

Jed Yeah, I really like it here, even the weather.

Elsa You don't miss the Aussie weather?

Jed We have to put on raincoats in Australia, too… In the winter. And I've got football here.

Lily And punting…remember?

Jed Oh, sure…

Lily Hey, do you know what you have to do? You really have to give a class presentation on Australia.

Jed I *so* don't have to do that!

b Correct the false sentences.

1 Jed says Australia has bad weather, too.

2 Jed likes Lily's presentation idea.

3 Alfie agrees with Jed.

4 Jed knows his grandma is coming to visit him.

2 a Spoken English **What do these expressions mean? How do you say them in your own language?**

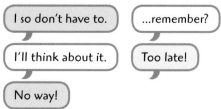

(I so don't have to.) (…remember?)

(I'll think about it.) (Too late!)

(No way!)

b In groups, practise reading out the dialogue.

▶ **Workbook** page 62, exercise 1

2

Lily Alfie, tell Jed to give the class a talk.

Alfie Jed, you must give the class a talk – what about?

Jed Australia. Alfie, tell the girls it isn't a good idea.

Alfie No way. I really think you should do it. What have you got to lose?

Jed My cool! I'll be embarrassed.

Elsa You're not that cool, Jed.

Lily Come on, you can do it!

Jed Well, I'll think about it…

Lily Anyway, it's too late. I told the teacher this morning.

Jed Lily!

3

Jed's mum What's the problem? Go on. Give it a try.

Jed Oh, Mum.

Jed's mum Don't give up now, before you start.

Jed I don't know enough to do a presentation.

Jed's mum You don't know enough about Australia to give a presentation to your class?

Jed But they want to hear about kangaroos, spiders and snakes…

Jed's mum Your grandma can help. She grew up in the outback.

Jed OK. I'll call her later. [*Doorbell*]

Jed's mum I think you should go and answer that.

Grandma Hi Jed. Surprise!

Jed Grandma!

3 a What do you think Jed does next and why?

b 🔊 **3.30** ▶ Now listen and check your ideas.

4 Over to you! Work with a partner. Answer the questions.

1 Would you be happy to give a talk to your class or school? Why? / Why not?

2 Was it bad that Lily made Jed do it?

3 Would you like a surprise visit from someone? Who?

Everyday English

Persuading and encouraging

5 a Look at the useful phrases. Find examples in the story.

Persuading

Go on. Give it a try.

I (don't) think you should (do it).

You (really) must do it.

You (really) have to…

What have you got to lose?

Encouraging

Come on, you can do it!

Don't give up!

b 🔊 **3.31** Listen and repeat.

▶ **Workbook** page 62, exercises 2–3

Pronunciation Silent letters

6 a 🔊 **3.32** Listen and repeat the words. Which letters are silent?

answer	know	right
school	should	talk	what
when	while	who	would

b Which of these words have silent letters?

fault	friend	must
mustn't	night	walk
want	weather	will

c 🔊 **3.33** Listen and check your answers.

▶ **Workbook** page 63, exercise 4

Listening and Speaking

7 a 🔊 **3.34** Listen to three conversations. What are the situations?

b 🔊 **3.34** Listen again. Who is persuading or encouraging? Are they successful? Check with a partner.

▶ **Workbook** page 63, exercises 5–7

8 a Get ready to speak Look at this list. How can you persuade or encourage your partner to try these things?

1 enter a photography competition

2 perform a rap song

3 make a huge cake

4 try spicy or unusual food

5 learn to play squash

6 finish a long race

b Work in pairs. Take turns to persuade / encourage each other. Role-play with a partner. Try different expressions. Use this chart to help you:

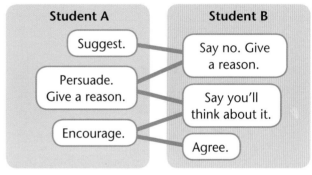

Student A	Student B
Suggest.	Say no. Give a reason.
Persuade. Give a reason.	Say you'll think about it.
Encourage.	Agree.

I think you should…

I really don't want to do that.
I don't like that sort of thing.

Go on, what have you got to lose?

c Role-play one of your dialogues for the class.

Persuade your family and friends to try out interesting new things. Give good reasons! Make short dialogues.

We really must try windsurfing! What do you think?

I'm not sure I fancy it.

Please… What have you got to lose?

Well, OK, but you have to help me!

Vocabulary Phrasal verbs

1 Complete the sentences with the correct particle from the box.

> down   for   off   on   up

1 It's hot in here. I'll take ___ my coat.
2 I can't see my book. Could you switch ___ the light?
3 Can you see Mum's glasses? She put them ___ somewhere in the room.
4 I'll turn ___ the volume. I can't hear it very well.
5 Help me look ___ my dictionary. I can't find it.

Adverbs -ly

2 Complete the sentences with the adjectives from the box in the correct form.

> careful   dangerous   happy   quiet   sad

1 He was crying and he said goodbye ___.
2 The children played on the beach ___.
3 'Shh!' she said, and she opened the door ___.
4 I wrote the birthday card ___.
5 They drove round the corner ___.

Grammar should / shouldn't

3 Write advice for these problems using should / shouldn't and the words in brackets.

1 I'm so tired. (bed)
2 I missed the bus. (sleep in)
3 I've got no money. (spend it all)
4 We're hungry. (sandwich)
5 I'm angry with my best friend. (talk to)

must / mustn't

4 Look at the signs and write the rules using must / mustn't.

have to / don't have to

5 Complete the dialogues with have to in the correct form.

1 A What ¹___ you ²___ do this evening?
   B I ³___ write my History essay.
2 A Why ⁴___ he ⁵___ go home so soon?
   B He ⁶___ look after his little sister.
3 A ⁷___ we ⁸___ finish the exercise now?
   B No, you ⁹___ do it now, but you ¹⁰___ finish it tomorrow.
4 A It's Sunday. We ¹¹___ wake up early. Hurray!
   B Yes, and we ¹²___ go to school!

Everyday English

Persuading and encouraging

6 Complete the dialogue with the words in the box.

> give up   must   think so   to lose

A I can't do this work. I'm going to fail.
B Don't ¹___ ! You're doing really well. You'll pass the exam.
A I don't ²___ . I'm no good at remembering things.
B You ³___ do it.
A Do you think I can pass?
B Yes, if you keep working. What have you got ⁴___ ?

Learning to learn
How do you learn best?

7 Look at this list and discuss it with a partner. Which do you do? Which do you not do? Which should you try to do in future?

1 Working by yourself in a quiet room.
2 Working with other students.
3 Going online and using a website or computer game.
4 Playing language games.
5 Learning rules.
6 Trying to always speak the language in class.

▶ **Workbook** pages 64–65, exercises 1–7

My project

What kind of stories do you watch or read? Why? Make a list and compare with the class.

Writing a story

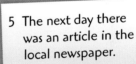

5 The next day there was an article in the local newspaper.

3 It was a lovely sunny day.

2 'Let's look up "plastic pollution" online.'

4 'This is terrible. We have to do something!'

6 They felt a bit nervous before the talk.

1 More than one hundred students marched down to the beach.

1 a You are going to write a story based on some pictures and text. Look at the pictures. Can you tell what the story is? Work with a partner and put the pictures in the correct order.

b Look at the sentences from Atish's project (1–6). Match them to the correct picture.

c Give the characters in the pictures names. Now write at least three sentences for each picture. You can use all or any of Atish's sentences, if you like.

d Add more detail to your story. Try to use adjectives and adverbs, and include interesting information, dialogue or description.

e How do you think the story ends? Write the end of the story. Choose any of these endings or make up your own.

They appear in the national news.

They start a website to organize beach clean-ups all over the country.

They start a website to raise money for plastic pollution projects.

They win an award.

A celebrity comes to visit them.

f Read everyone's stories. Which one has the best…

adverbs? descriptions? dialogue? ending?

What is Australia famous for? Make notes in pairs. Tell the class.

FACT FILE

Name: The Commonwealth of ¹___
Flag: The Southern Cross
Capital: ²___
Largest city: ³___
Population: ⁴___
Currency: Australian ⁵___
Language: ⁶___
Weather: Summer – hot and sunny. Winter – ⁷___ and ⁸___
Sport: Australian ⁹___

AUSTRALIA

Jed's 'A Bit of Geography'

Australia is the sixth largest country in the world. It's the only country that is also a continent.

A third of Australia is desert. We call it the 'outback'. But we also have tropical rainforests.

Australia's wildlife is unusual. Australia is the world's largest island continent, so we have animals that are completely different to the rest of the world, e.g. kangaroos and koala bears. We also have the best collection of poisonous animals and insects – we have 36 types of poisonous spider, and 20 types of poisonous snake!

Two famous natural places are Uluru, also known as Ayer's Rock, one of the biggest rocks in the world, and the Great Barrier Reef – the world's biggest coral reef.

Jed's 'A Bit of History'

Aboriginal people arrived in Australia about 50,000 years ago. They came from Asia when sea levels were lower. They learned to live in the hot weather of the outback.

Explorers from the Netherlands first landed in Australia in 1606. The British arrived in 1770 and were the first to live there in 1788. The British government sent a lot of prisoners there!

At first, the new people lived peacefully with the Aboriginal people. But then they had fights over land.

In 1851, people discovered gold in Australia. So, thousands of new people arrived to try to find gold and become rich. In 1901 the six separate regions in Australia all joined together as one country with the new national flag.

1 a Work with a partner. Look at the fact file. Which information can you complete before you listen to Jed's talk?

b 🔊 **3.35** Listen to Jed's talk and complete the fact file.

2 a Work in pairs. Read your information. Make notes under the correct headings and share with your partner.

Student A Read Jed's 'A Bit of Geography'.
Student B Read Jed's 'A Bit of History'.

Size	Aboriginal people
Continent	Explorers landed
Wildlife	When the British arrived
Famous natural places	Finding gold

b What was the most interesting fact in each text? What new things did you learn about Australia?

3 Over to you! Write a short presentation with information about your country or your favourite country. Work in groups. Discuss as a class.

 New Zealand

Learn through English

What types of renewable energy do you know? Do you know anyone who uses any of them?

RENEWABLE ENERGY

ENERGY SOLUTIONS
THE NUMBERS

In ¹____, the biggest solar farm in the country is on a sheep farm. Thousands of solar panels make ᵃ____ million hours of electricity a year. They also protect the sheep from sun and rain!

The world's biggest wind turbines are off the coast of ²____. Their blades are bigger than the London Eye! One turn powers a house for ᵇ____ hours!

³____'s Three Gorges dam is the biggest dam in the world. It took ᶜ____ years to build. It is the country that makes the most electricity from hydropower.

⁴____ has a lot of volcanoes which produce hot water and air. So ᵈ____ % of the country's electricity comes from geothermal energy. It's very cheap!

⁵____ grows the most biofuels, usually corn. Most cars there can use ᵉ____ % vegetable fuel mixed with oil. Many cars can just use biofuel.

RENEWABLE ENERGY

We use mostly oil, gas and coal for our energy around the world. This causes pollution and global warming. These are two huge problems. So, we have to change our energy supply. The world's scientists have given us renewable energy and we should use more of it.

1 a What types of renewable energy can you see in the photos?

b Complete the definitions with the words below and match them to the photos (A–E).

> biofuel   geothermal energy
> hydropower   solar power   wind power

Types of Renewable Energy
1 ____ – using heat from the sun to make electricity
2 ____ – using wind to make electricity or to make machines work
3 ____ – using water to make electricity
4 ____ – using heat from the earth to make electricity or to make hot water
5 ____ – using plants, not oil, to make machines work

2 a Read about different countries using renewable energy and try to complete gaps 1–5 with the countries in the box.

> Australia   Britain   China   Iceland   The USA

b Complete gaps a–e with the numbers in the box.

> 1   10   29   30   200

c 🔊 3.36 Listen and check. Write the numbers you hear for the correct country.

d Which information do you find the most interesting?

3 Over to you! What renewable energies does your country use? Find out and tell the class. Do you know any problems with renewable energy? Discuss.

1 🔊 3.37 ▶ Read and listen to the story.

Unit 1, Speaking, p11

| clean | close | organize | pin | put | throw | tidy | write |

Unit 2, Speaking and Listening, p21

1

cloudy
forest
walk

2

a bush
start / rain
stop / rain
wait
want

3

Boxer
decide
hike in the mountains
Jack
Jane
sunny

Unit 3, Speaking, p37

Student A's shopping list
some bread
some chocolate
some milk
some strawberries
some yoghurt

Unit 4, Speaking, p51

YOU HAVE CHOSEN

CASTLE   DESERT   FOREST   LAKE

Unit 5, Listening and Speaking, p65

Student A

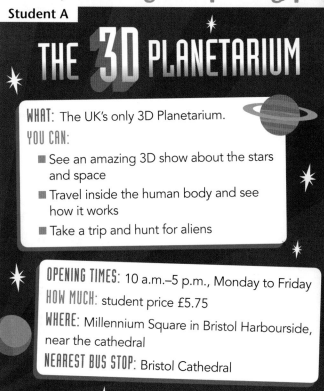

THE 3D PLANETARIUM

WHAT: The UK's only 3D Planetarium.
YOU CAN:

- See an amazing 3D show about the stars and space
- Travel inside the human body and see how it works
- Take a trip and hunt for aliens

OPENING TIMES: 10 a.m.–5 p.m., Monday to Friday
HOW MUCH: student price £5.75
WHERE: Millennium Square in Bristol Harbourside, near the cathedral
NEAREST BUS STOP: Bristol Cathedral

Unit 6, Listening and Speaking, p77

Student A
You want to arrange a time to go to the cinema.
The film starts at 7 p.m. Here's your diary:

Monday	Science revision all evening for test
Tuesday	music club 6–8 p.m.
Wednesday	aunt and uncle's house for dinner
Thursday	
Friday	hockey training 6–8 p.m.
Saturday	hockey match 1 p.m. kick off
Sunday	lunch with grandparents

Unit 1, Speaking, p11

clean   close   organize   pin   put   throw   tidy   write

Unit 2, Speaking and Listening, p21

finish
home
hurry
storm

a cave
follow
safe
stay

a storm
bark
Boxer
dangerous
scary
show

Unit 3, Speaking, p37

Student B's shopping list
some apples
some cans of cola
some carrots
some eggs
some juice
some milk

Unit 4, Speaking, p51

YOU HAVE CHOSEN

| JUNGLE | MOUNTAIN | PALACE | SEA |

Unit 5, Listening and Speaking, p65

Student B

THE AQUARIUM

WHAT: An underwater aquarium in the centre of the city.

YOU CAN:
▶ Watch amazing and fascinating sea life
▶ Feed our Giant Pacific Octopus
▶ Be scared by our exhibition on river monsters!

OPENING TIMES: 10 a.m.–5 p.m., every day
HOW MUCH: student price £9.75
WHERE: Millennium Square in Bristol Harbourside, near the cathedral
NEAREST BUS STOP: Bristol Cathedral

Unit 6, Listening and Speaking, p77

Student B
You want to arrange a time to finish your art project together. You need about four hours. Here's your diary:

Monday	dentist 4 p.m.
Tuesday	music club 6–8 p.m.
Wednesday	
Thursday	photography club 3–5 p.m.
Friday	tennis
Saturday	tennis 10 a.m.–12 p.m.
Sunday	look after cousins 2–5 p.m.

OXFORD
UNIVERSITY PRESS

Great Clarendon Street, Oxford, OX2 6DP, United Kingdom

Oxford University Press is a department of the University of Oxford.
It furthers the University's objective of excellence in research, scholarship,
and education by publishing worldwide. Oxford is a registered trade
mark of Oxford University Press in the UK and in certain other countries

ISBN: 978 0 19 425557 1 4

Printed in China

This book is printed on paper from certified and well-managed sources

ACKNOWLEDGEMENTS

Based on an original concept by Tom Hutchinson

The Best Detective in Town? by: Paul Shipton (pp.32–33, 58–59, 84–85)

*The authors and publishers are very grateful to all the teachers who have offered their
comments and suggestions which have been invaluable in the development of Project
Explore. We would particularly like to mention those who have helped by commenting on
Project Explore:*

Croatia: Alenka Poropat, Mirta Grizak Štrbenac

Czech Republic: Barbora Krpcová, Soňa Jindrová

Hungary: Pintérné Gyarmati Anikó, Illés Gabriella

Serbia: Jagoda Popovic, Vojislava Koljević

Slovakia: Marcel Prievozník, David Ručka

Slovenia: Andreja Hazabent, Vojko Jurgec

Front cover photograph by: Mike Stone.

Back cover photograph: Oxford University Press building/David Fisher

Commissioned photography by: MM Studios

Illustrations by: Ray and Corinne Burrow/Beehive Illustration p.55; Hennie
Hayworth/Meiklejohn p.61; Vlado Krizan/Good Illustration pp.50, 51, 86 (Unit
4), 87 (Unit 4); Andrew Painter pp.5, 17, 38, 49, 74; Dusan Pavlic/Beehive
Illustration pp.13, 28, 35, 37, 42, 43, 60, 64, 68, 75, 80; Jeremy Pyke/Advocate
Art pp.47, 57 (couple with computers), 67, 69, 71; Ben Scruton/Meiklejohn
pp.20, 81, 86 (Unit 2), 87 (Unit 2); Simon Smith/Beehive Illustration pp.10, 36,
86 (Unit 1), 87 (Unit 1); Amit Tayal/Beehive Illustration pp.32, 33, 58, 59, 84, 85;
Tim Wesson/Meiklejohn p.72.

The publisher would like to thank the following for permission to reproduce photographs:
123rf: pp.24 (flood/federicofoto), 49 (Chrissie/Olga Volodina), 82 (Australian
outback/Tero Hakala); Alamy Stock Photo: pp.30 (Gertrude Bell portrait/
Chronicle, Gertrude Bell on a picnic/Vintage Archives), 31 (scientists/Avalon/
Photoshot License), 56 (1940s computer/INTERFOTO, Analytical Engine/Photo
12), 60 (Imperial War Museum interior/Pawel Libera Images), 62 (ferry/allan
wright), 70 (Snowdon and lake/David Noton Photography, walker on Snowdon
summit/Image Source Salsa), 76 (lionesses/Polly Thomas), 83 (hydropower/
Xinhua, wind power/Tony West); Bridgeman Images: p.19 (Rik with a black eye
patch, 1915 (oil on canvas), Wouters, Rik (1882–1916)/Koninklijk Museum voor
Schone Kunsten, Antwerp, Belgium/© Lukas – Art in Flanders VZW/Bridgeman
Images, Self Portrait (w/c on paper) (see also 183575), Stillman, Marie Spartali
(1844–1927)/Private Collection/Photo © The Maas Gallery, London/Bridgeman
Images, Self portrait in a Turban with her Child, 1786 (panel), Vigee-Lebrun,
Elisabeth Louise (1755–1842)/Louvre, Paris, France/Bridgeman Images; Getty
Images: pp.22 (jaguar/Photocech/iStock, lightening/Layne Kennedy/Corbis
Documentary), 29 (Pele/AFP), 44 (Jamie Oliver signing autographs/Daniel
Berehulak), 47 (IBM Simon/CARL COURT/AFP), 48 (games console/luismmolina/
E+), 56 (IBM Simon/Rob Stothard, IBM PC Model 5150 with printer/Science &
Society Picture Library, microchip/Science & Society Picture Library), 76 (Glen
James/Matthew J.Lee/The Boston Globe, street/Suzanne Kreiter The Boston
Globe/), 83 (solar power/Christopher Groenhout/Lonely Planet Images);
Oxford University Press: pp.12 (boy/Mark Bassett), 23 (Cloe, Maria, walkers
in snow), 39 (girl/Mark Bassett), 49 (Mia/Gareth Boden), 62 (map/Martin
Sanders/Beehive), 71 (tablet/Gianni Dagli Orti/Corbis); Shutterstock: pp.17,
29, 43, 55, 69, 81 (communication background/windweel), 9 (Arina P Habich),
12 (Chicago/Joseph Sohm, skiing/frantic00, Falaise/Pack-Shot, girl with
camera/mantinoc, toucan/Oleksiy Mark), 13 (Melbourne/Andrew Bertuleit,
splash/Left Handed Photography), 16 (Yuri Shevtsov), 18 (Buckingham Palace
exterior/Ewelina Wachala), Buckingham Palace interior, The White House
exterior/Orhan Cam, The White House interior/Evan Vucci/AP), 19 (Van
Gogh/Universal History Archive/Universal Images Group), 21 (Esther Pueyo),
22 (Amazon river/Johnny Lye), 23 (Anton/Monkey Business Images, Bob/
Gelpi, canoeing/Chaisit Rattanachusri, pyramids/Brian Kinney, rainforest/
Quick Shot, Tatra mountains/PHOTOCREO Michal Bednarek, The Nile/WitR,
Paris/Sean Hsu, tourists/nd3000), 24 (avalanche/Lysogor Roman, Earth/BEST-
BACKGROUNDS, earthquake/Naypong Studio, hurricane/Drew McArthur,
lightning/Fesus Robert, snowstorm/Zoran Ras, tornado/solarseven, volcano/
Rainer Albiez, wave/Mana Photo), 25 (boy/Tracy Whiteside, damaged house/
Dustie), 26 (dog/Kristina Stasiuliene, lightening/Kucher Serhii), 27 (Stefano
Carocci PH), 29 (Christ the Redeemer Statue/Mark Schwettmann, Copacabana
beach/Aleksandar Todorovic, Sugar Loaf Mountain/R.M. Nunes), 30 (David
Livingstone/Granger, Victoria Falls/Przemyslaw Skibinski), 31 (Arctic Petrel/
Alexey Seafarer, penguins/axily, Robert Scott/Granger, tourist boat/Katiekk),
34 (bananas/Maks Narodenko, cheese/azure1, chicken/Yellow Cat, chocolate/
Nikola Bilic, coffee/Viktor1, cola/M.Unal Ozmen, crisps/Dawid Rojek, eggs/
KIM NGUYEN, grapes/Sailorr, ham/Annetua, lamb chops/Robyn Mackenzie,
lemonade/Hortimages, milk/SOMMAI, orange juice/Mariusz Szczygiel,
pasta/bergamont, potatoes/Nattika, rice/SOMMAI, sandwich/GMEVIPHOTO,
strawberries/ravi, tea/gresel, yoghurt/MaraZe), 38 (apple pie/D. Pimborough,
cola/nednapa, fish/AS Food studio, toast/Lisa S.), 39 (jogger/Spectral-Design),
44 (Jamie Oliver cooking/Ross Hogson, Jamie Oliver outside 15/Jonathan
Player), 45 (girl with smartphone/Africa Studio, skipping/progressman, smart
watch/Andrey_Popov, virtual realty game/Nikodash), 46 (camera eye/Vladimir
Sukhachev, charger/de2marco, games consol/Colin Hui, keyboard/rangizzz,
laptop/zentilia, printer/Adisa, router/DR-Images, tablet/Oleksiy Mark),
48 (3D printer/Alexander Tolstykh, driverless car/metamorworks, drone/
akiyoko, e-reader/Petar Djordjevic, earphones/ang intaravichian, electric car/
Zapp.2Photo, Franky Zapata/CHRISTIAN MERZ/EPA-EFE, smartphone/fetrinka,
smartwatch/dolphfyn, VR headset/Mark Nazh), 49 (Harry/RimDream), 53 (Alex
Staroseltsev), 54 (camera eye/Vladimir Sukhachev, charger/de2marco, games
consol/Colin Hui, keyboard/rangizzz, laptop/zentilia, printer/Adisa, router/
DR-Images, tablet/Oleksiy Mark), 56 (Alan Turing/Granger), 57 (connecting
to internet/Macrovector, world online learning/JuliRose), 60 (fountain/Alex
Gorins, National Portrait Gallery interior/Alex Segre, Westminster Cathedral
interior/Kit Leong), 62 (children/Darren Baker, coastline Rum/Iain Frazer,
dolphins/Chanonry), 63 (Antarctica/Alexy Suloev, boy/MarKord , Burj Khalifa/
Laborant, girl/Darren Baker), 65 (stocker1970), 69 (cream tea/Monkey Business
Images, Kingsbridge/James Dale), 70 (bison/Steve Boice, caldera/Wisanu
Boonrawd, geyser/Poul Riishede, Snowdon railway/stocker1970), 71 (map/
KajzrPhotography, ziggurat/Simon Edge), 73 (boy/Sabphoto), 76 (flames/J.
Helgason, growling lioness/Johan Swanepoel, rucksack/ElRoi), 77 (football
match/makieni), 82 (globe/Atakan Yildiz, Great Barrier Reef/Brian Kinney,
kangaroo/IntoTheWorld), 83 (corn/smereka, geothermal/sapikusan).